Ephesians

Chosen in Christ

John M. Fowler

REVIEW AND HERALD® PUBLISHING ASSOCIATION
HAGERSTOWN, MD 21740

The author assumes full responsibility for the accuracy of all facts and quotations as cited in this book.

This book was
Edited by Raymond H. Woolsey
Copyedited by James Cavil and Delma Miller
Designed by Trent Truman
Cover art by Justinen Creative Group
Typeset: Bembo 11/13

PRINTED IN U.S.A.

09 08 07 06 05 5 4 3 2 1

R&H Cataloging Service
Fowler, John M. 1939- .
Ephesians: Chosen in Him.

1. Bible. N. T. Ephesians—Criticism, interpretation, etc. I. Title

227.5

ISBN 0-8280-1885-5

To D. S. David,

my first pastor,

who introduced me to the riches of God's Word,

and modeled a ministry

and a leadership

that recognized no middle wall of partition.

Also by
John M. Fowler:
Cosmic Conflict Between Christ and Satan

To order, call
1-800-765-6955.
Visit us at
www.reviewandherald.com
for information on other Review and Herald® products.

Contents

Introduction

"We shall now separate for the ordinance of humility."

The preacher finished the announcement. The procession to the service of foot washing began as usual—men to the right, women to the left, worshippers choosing their partners as they made their way to the basins. One man at the rear of the church caught my attention. He had come late for the service, sat on the floor, listened intently to the sermon, and taken seriously the invitation that all who have accepted Jesus could participate in the open Communion that Adventists celebrate. But he was new to the church. He knew no one. And he eagerly waited for someone to invite him to be a partner in preparation for Communion. He seemed poor, friendless, and on the wrong side of the caste line. His position appeared to be desperate to himself and embarrassing to the saints in that small-town church in a country where caste still defines community.

I looked intently at the agony etched on the face of the visitor. I waited prayerfully for the universality of the gospel to break forth like dawn's first rays. Which of the saints would offer to be partner to this man? The elders were busy organizing the details. The deacons were busy fetching water from the only faucet outside the church. Others kept to themselves, as though the visitor was not their concern. After all, the Levites and the priests are extremely busy people, not to be disturbed by trivia.

Suddenly the visitor did have a partner: Ravi Anandan. Ravi knelt on the cold concrete floor, gently cradled his partner's shoeless, dusty feet, and washed them in the clear, cool water, which instantly turned to a muddy brown. One month ago Ravi would have done no such thing. He would not have allowed even the shadow of that man to come anywhere near him. Touching him would have been touching the untouchable, and touching the untouchable was an act of religious impurity and social repugnance.

What made Ravi pull down the barrier and extend the embrace? Ravi had accepted Jesus and discovered the joy of redemption. He had learned that part of that joy is to know Jesus. Another part is to accept his fellow humans as equal to himself, thus experiencing the family of God. As he continued to study the New Testament, Ravi was deeply moved by the image of the broken wall in Paul's Epistle to the Ephesians. He learned that in Jesus Christ every wall of partition comes crumbling down and a new humanity arises for the glory of God. A new conviction took hold of him—if he wanted to be part of Christ's new humanity, he had to follow Jesus fully and let those walls in his life come down.

Walls or Jesus? It had to be one or the other, not both. Ravi chose Jesus over the walls of which he had once been proud. And now at the Lord's table, Ravi stepped across the age-old barrier of caste and prejudice and affirmed his newfound faith. With the courage of this faith he shattered the walls within and reached out to touch the untouchable.

That newness, that embrace, that unity in Christ, is what makes the Epistle to Ephesians a gospel of new relationships. Theologians and commentators alike see in this Epistle God's order in a chaotic world, God's unified community in a world of disintegration, God's ultimate message of reconciliation in the midst of alienation, and God's victory over satanic forces of discord and disruption. Ephesians was John Calvin's favorite letter. William Barclay calls it "the queen of Epistles." Charles Dodd sees in it "the crown of Paulinism." Edgar Goodspeed finds it a "rhapsody on the worth of . . . salvation."

We can study the Epistle for its theology, ecclesiology, or Christian sociology, but one thing we cannot escape: Paul's confidence in the new creation God has wrought in Christ and its ultimate triumph in the great controversy. From God's choice of us from "before the foundation of the world" (Eph. 1:4) to the battle against the "spiritual hosts of wickedness" (Eph. 6:12) the Epistle resonates with the power of grace, prayer, and faith.

It is with that spirit of prayer that we must approach the study of this Epistle of new relationships. As we do, may we also understand the mystery and majesty of that power that motivated Ravi to reach out and touch what he once deemed untouchable. May we experience for ourselves that life-changing power so that in Christ we too shall be true members of His new creation, forgiven of our sins, reconciled to God, and related to one another with every wall of separation demolished forever.

CHAPTER 1

The Church at Ephesus

During the time of Paul, Ephesus was considered the fourth-largest city of the Roman Empire, following Rome, Alexandria, and Antioch of Pisidia. Situated on the banks of the Cayster River as it flowed into the Aegean Sea, it was once a thriving port, on the main road from Rome to eastern Asia. This strategic location made the city a commercial, political, banking, and religious center of western Asia and the home for large Greek, Roman, and Jewish communities. The city's greatest attraction, however, was not its Greek philosophy, its Roman jurisprudence, or its economic wealth, but its religion.

The city's religion revolved around the cult of Diana, the goddess of fertility, whom "all Asia and the world" worshipped at that time (Acts 19:27). Known as Artemis of Ephesus, the goddess made the city the largest tourist attraction of Asia Minor. Its worship and the temple's physical grandeur were a great source of the city's wealth.

At the height of its popularity the Temple of Diana was considered one of the Seven Wonders of the Ancient World. Built of solid marble and lined with gold, the temple was massive in structure. It measured 425 by 225 feet and comprised 127 columns, each 60 feet high, displaying carved images of life-size figures.

Into this city, absorbed so passionately with the worship of the deity of fertility (Acts 19:24, 25), Paul came proclaiming, "They are not gods which are made with hands" (verse 26). The apostle's message struck at the very foundation of the belief system and lifestyle of Ephesus.

Christ or Diana?

Christ or Diana? The question is as old as the great controversy between Christ and Satan. On the one hand is the Creator, and on the other a creature. Between the Creator and the creature, to whom will our allegiance be? Satan's cunningness has crafted Dianas in many shapes and forms, and we meet them at every turn of life's journey. We meet them in our homes, where the sanctity of marriage is often held in scorn, where the Word of God is neglected, where children are left to fend on their own, and where the centrality of Christ is exchanged for the elevation of self. We see them in our schools and colleges, where education aims to develop the ideal person who will embrace and live by the values of humanism. We meet Dianas in business, politics, and social ethos, where success defines one's values and norms, where a lie is no longer a lie but only a statement made under duress and viewed out of context, where the violation of the seventh commandment must be viewed in terms of whether the act was done with consent.

Thus Dianas are not limited to idols. Whatever competes with, or replaces, the God who created and His unique revelation in Christ is a Diana that stands in the way of the gospel taking full effect on human life. One need not seek Diana in other religious systems; she is within and not far away from the human heart and mind. Against all such Dianas stands the gospel of Jesus Christ that Paul introduced in Ephesus, laying the foundation of one of the finest churches of New Testament times.

Ephesus: the Beginnings of the Church

Paul's first visit to Ephesus was a brief one. As he came to the conclusion of his second missionary journey, making his way from Corinth to Jerusalem, the apostle, who would not give up any available opportunity to preach the good news of Jesus, stopped at the port city of Ephesus (Acts 18:19) and preached the gospel to the Jews in their synagogue. He found a receptive spirit.

His audience was so impressed that they requested him to stay a little longer, but he declined because of his commitment to be in Jerusalem for the upcoming festivals. But the apostle must have sensed a great potential for Ephesus to become an ideal launching pad for the gospel of Christ all over Asia Minor. He left behind Aquila and Priscilla to nurture the work he had just begun, and promised he would return, "God willing."

Ephesus means "desirable." Before Paul and his companions arrived in the city it was desirable for the worship of Diana. It was desirable for sin and its varied allurements. But the entry of the gospel was to turn the city into a desirable one for an entirely different reason. A belief system built around Diana would be confronted by the God of creation, who dwells in heavenly places and has now revealed Himself through Jesus Christ. A city plagued by divisions of race, language, culture, and economic status was to experience the wonder of unity and oneness.

Where Christ is, there is change—from falsehood to truth, from superstition to reality, from corrupt and perverse lifestyle to holy and sanctified calling, and from division to unity. With that change, Ephesus became a truly desirable city and gave birth to a church about which the ascended Jesus would say through John, "I know your works, your labor, your patience, and that you cannot bear those who are evil" (Rev. 2:2).

Aquila and Priscilla, converts of Paul and tentmakers like him, refugees from persecution in Rome, became the first ministers of the small group of believers in Ephesus. Their life and ministry illustrate God's plan for the nurture of the church. It is God's intention, not that every congregation should have a full-time ordained minister, but that every person who has accepted the gospel be a proclaimer and a nurturer of the good news.

In addition to Aquila and Priscilla, the church at Ephesus had the blessing of the ministry of Apollos, a Jew from Alexandria and a convert to the message of John the Baptist. Learned in Greek philosophy, eloquent in speech, well versed in Scripture, Apollos "had been instructed in the way of the Lord; and being fervent in spirit, he spoke and taught accurately the things of the Lord" (Acts 18:25). His skills in oratory and his education in philosophy did not turn him into an educated snob. Apollos was humble enough to submit himself to the Scriptures. That humble spirit led him to accept the call for repentance, and he became a follower of the Baptist. Later he turned into an itinerant preacher, convincing Jews from city to city that Jesus Christ was the Messiah.

When Apollos came and preached in Ephesus, in his audience were Aquila and Priscilla. They perceived that Apollos was a godly man, obedient to the Scriptures, and devoted to the spread of its message. But they also noticed that Apollos knew "only the baptism of John" (verse 25) and was not aware of the fullness of truth. Nor was he aware of the work of the Holy Spirit.

Aquila and Priscilla noted in him a potential defender and proclaimer of the gospel for the emerging church, and they sought him out privately "and explained to him the way of God more accurately" (verse 26). As a result, "the educated orator received instruction from them with grateful surprise and joy. Through their teachings he obtained a clearer understanding of the Scriptures, and became one of the ablest defenders of the Christian church."[1]

From then on Apollos became so powerful a defender and preacher of the gospel in Ephesus, Corinth, and other cities of Asia that Paul acknowledged his effectiveness as a minister and included him with Peter and himself as faithful sowers, nurturers, and reapers of the gospel harvest (1 Cor. 1:12).

Thus, early in its life, the Ephesian church became a learning center, a witnessing outlet, and a prime example of the unity and love that should exist among believers. The risen Jesus "used [this church] as a symbol of the entire Christian church in the apostolic age."[2]

Paul's Ministry at Ephesus

Paul returned to Ephesus during his third missionary journey. This time he spent nearly three years preaching, teaching, cultivating, and building a strong center for Christ, because of which "all who dwelt in Asia heard the word of the Lord Jesus, both Jews and Greeks" (Acts 19:10).

Jews and Greeks. Right at the outset of his long pastoral ministry, Paul wanted his followers to know that the gospel of Jesus Christ has no frontiers and does not play favorites. Christ is the Savior of all people, regardless of their color, ethnicity, life status, gender, or whatever divisive factor sin has introduced into human life. He is the Lord of all. This message would ring through all the Epistles of the apostle to the Gentiles, particularly in Ephesians.

Paul's long ministry at Ephesus began with the right note—bringing the fullness of truth to the first believers in the city. As in the case of Apollos, these believers had received the baptism of John but not of Jesus, and had not even "heard whether there is a Holy Spirit" (verse 2).

What was so important about baptism in the name of Jesus? For one thing, the baptism of John was a call to repentance, a preparatory step to believing "on Him who would come after him, that is, on Christ Jesus" (verse 4). Any truth that does not lead to Jesus or that contradicts Jesus cannot be truth at all. Jesus is not an option on a menu of different avenues to truth, all considered by some as equally valid and objectively effective. His claims are unique; He has no competitor. To be baptized in the name of Jesus is to receive the redemption that comes from Him and to declare a permanent allegiance to the One who said, "I am the way, the truth, and the life. No one comes to the Father except through Me" (John 14:6). John the Baptist could not be that way. Nor the prophets. Nor Diana. Nor any of those "gods many, and lords many (1 Cor. 8:5, KJV)."

When the nucleus of first believers accepted that Jesus is the Lord, they indeed took the step of full acceptance—they were baptized in the name of Jesus. The believers received the Holy Spirit and "spoke with tongues and prophesied" (Acts 19:6). The sign of receiving the Holy Spirit is not the same in all instances, and it is not fair to place speaking in tongues and prophesying as the tests of having the Spirit.

The Bible records other signs of being blessed by the Spirit. Walking in accordance to God's law (Eze. 36:27); presenting oneself as God's temple (1 Cor. 3:16); being power-filled witnesses to Christ (Acts 1:8); living uprightly as God's children (Rom. 8:14-16); accepting all humans as God's children (Acts 10:19, 29); and living the life of Christ (Rom. 8:11) are some of the signs of being filled with the Holy Spirit. No miracle is greater than the miracle of a changed, transformed life.

The first church at Ephesus had only 12 men (Acts 19:7). Even if there also were some women and children, it was by no means a large church. But an evangelist who has sensed his or her commission from the Lord will not and must not count the success of his or her mission by the number of people baptized. Evangelism is not a number game but an event of proclamation.

For three months Paul preached in the synagogue, trying to show to the Jews that Jesus is the fulfillment of the Old Testament prophecies and that He indeed is the Messiah and the Savior of the world. While some Jews believed, many—Greeks as well as Jews—were not ready to accept the inclusive nature of the gospel of Jesus, and Paul had to withdraw from the synagogue to a school. How odd that a synagogue should reject the preaching of the gospel, while a secular place of learning welcomes the hearing of the newly entered truth. Paul preached there continually for two years.

Church growth requires patient and continuous nurture. When Willis Lowry arrived in the 1940s in the northeastern hill state of Mizoram, India, there were no other Adventists in the area. His wife, Helen, and he were the first missionaries, and they knew the work before them would be as arduous and rough as those hills and the tribes that lived among them. But they were determined that their first commitment was to the faithful proclamation of the Advent message.

Mizoram had hardly any roads, not much of a health or education system, or political stability. The Lowrys lived among the people, made friends with them, shared what little they had, and slowly began to speak of their faith. They visited nearby villages on foot or on horseback, making friends and influencing people.

Helen was an excellent cook, and although she did not have the ingredients to exhibit the best of her talents, she made good use of whatever was available. This impressed the women of the community. Willis had big hands to help, a large heart to empathize, and a perpetual smile that helped him make friends easily. With these talents they contextualized the gospel, learned the local language, and taught the people.

Willis would not baptize anyone until that person knew the gospel in every detail and had practiced it for weeks. Sometimes it took nearly six months for a person to be ready for baptism. The church grew rather slowly. There were no mass baptisms. Members felt a sense of ownership of the church and its program. The strongest laity-led evangelism and nurture program in the Southern Asia Division characterized the church and set it on a path to maturity. Mizoram became one field where auditors were seldom needed, where politics were at a minimum, and where the study of the Bible and the Spirit of Prophecy became a passionate preoccupation.

As a result, 60 years later the church in Mizoram registered not only a steady nurture and solid growth but also the highest percentage of per capita giving. This eventually qualified the mission to become the first conference in that division.

That's the kind of nurture Paul gave to Ephesus. The apostle spent three years in that city, but they were not easy years. He saw the gospel polarize the city between the crucified and risen Jesus and the lifeless Diana. At one time the entire city erupted in riots against Paul and his fellow preachers. The worshippers and priests of Diana were concerned not so much for their goddess as for their income. The city's merchants and labor guilds found that they had too much to lose if Diana was replaced by Jesus. They did not want to see the city's cash flow plummet and the unemployment rate of silversmiths and craftsmen rise. They would rather drive Paul and Jesus out (Acts 19:23-29).

Despite such opposition, Paul taught and preached, performing "unusual miracles" (verse 11). Those who believed in the gospel confessed their sins and turned from their ways of magic and sorcery. The world of the occult was shattered. The believers had a bonfire in the city, burning books devoted to Diana worth "several million dollars" (verse 19, NLT). Most important, the "word of the Lord grew mightily and prevailed" (verse 20).

A Strong Church

Among all the churches that the apostle Paul established, Ephesus seemed very close and special to him. After all, he had given three of his best and tumultuous years to the development of that church. When he had finished his third missionary journey and was heading back to Jerusalem, he wanted to meet the elders of Ephesus. Since his boat's itinerary included a stop at Miletus, some 30 miles from Ephesus, he summoned the church elders there for a farewell meeting. One has only to read his farewell message to the elders, in Acts 20:17-37, to understand his love and concern for the Ephesian church. But the farewell address has other important implications for pastors, evangelists, and church leaders of all times.

• A pastor's life must be as transparent and open as his or her ministry (verse 18).

• Ministry should be marked with humility and sincerity (verse 19).

• A pastor must be a teacher, teaching the truth in all its fullness, and holding back nothing that will edify the parishioner (verse 20).

• Such preaching and teaching must be Christ-centered—"repentance toward God and faith toward our Lord Jesus Christ"—and aim to unify all people in the oneness of Christ (verse 21).

• Service must come before self (verses 24-26). Paul's criterion for measuring life is how much is spent in the ministry of Jesus (verse 24).

• Ministry is not a one-person show. Paul believed in delegating responsibility (verses 28-31).

• The life of the church is often a life in a continuous crisis, from within and without. Pastors need to be aware of this—their life and message must continually address these crises and strengthen the flock (verses 29-31).

After such a careful and moving address, Paul prayed with the elders and left for Jerusalem, never to return to the church he loved so dearly. As all good evangelists should, the apostle left the stewardship of the church under the care of competent leaders (verse 28). Later the apostle appointed Timothy to minister there, with a special commission to ensure that the Ephesians "teach no other doctrine, nor give heed to fables and endless genealogies, which cause disputes rather than godly edification which is in faith" (1 Tim. 1:3, 4). The Ephesian church also had the privilege of the ministry and counsel of the beloved disciple John.[3]

Such was the birth and growth of the church at Ephesus. The church and the city have long since gone, but the love and the care that the apostle Paul had for it remains in the form of the Epistle he wrote to his beloved believers. The Epistle stands as a symbol of the unified relations that the apostle wished among all peoples who take up the name of Jesus.

---

[1] *The Seventh-day Adventist Bible Commentary* (Washington, D.C.: Review and Herald Pub. Assn., 1980), vol. 6, p. 1063.

[2] Ellen G. White, *The Acts of the Apostles* (Mountain View, Calif.: Pacific Press Pub. Assn., 1911), p. 578.

[3] *Ibid.*

Chapter 2

Themes in Ephesians

You "will see my face no more" (Acts 20:25). With those sorrowful words the apostle Paul took leave of the Ephesian elders gathered at Miletus. How prophetic those words proved to be. Paul was arrested in Jerusalem and eventually imprisoned in Rome. With his public work cut off, the apostle sat in Caesar's prison. He was not the one to brood over life's clouds; he took advantage of the quietness of the jail to ponder over the long road from Damascus to Rome.

The apostle would turn the liability of prison into a historic asset and a legacy to generations yet unborn. So he took time to write four important letters, called the Prison Epistles. Each one has a unique message. He wrote to Philemon on a very sensitive matter about his slave Onesimus, who had escaped to Rome and later had been converted by Paul. Calling Onesimus his son, Paul appeals to Philemon to accept him as a brother. An escaped slave worthy of death became a partner in the Christian family. Such is the power of the gospel of Christ.

The apostle wrote to the Colossians to save them from a heresy that questioned the very foundation of Christian faith, namely, the divinity of Christ and His incarnation. He also wrote an Epistle to the Philippians, the theme of which is joy in Christian brotherhood.

And he did not forget the church where he had spent three years. The Epistle to the Ephesians can be read for its doctrine of the church, for its worldview, for its doctrine of Christ, and for its doctrine of salvation by grace alone. But the primary focus of the Epistle is Christ the reconciler—the one who reconciles God and humanity, and the one who abolishes all the walls of brokenness between people, bringing about the unity envisioned at Creation.

The Author: the Apostle Paul

The author introduces himself as "Paul, an apostle of Jesus Christ by the will of God" (Eph. 1:1). Although the title "apostle" is initially applied in the Gospels to the 12 disciples, Paul also lays claim to the title. His claim arises not out of self-authentication but from absolute wonder. He knew with certainty that the risen Jesus had indeed confronted him personally on the road to Damascus and called him to be an apostle to the Gentiles (Acts 9:15), a fact that Peter and other apostles freely recognized (Gal. 2:8-10). But his wonder at such a call is Why would a Pharisee of the Pharisees, one who had fully dedicated himself to the destruction of the early church and on whose hands was the blood of numerous Christians (Acts 8:1; 9:1, 2), be called to be an apostle of Jesus Christ? The answer is God's grace.

Human genius cannot find an explanation for the workings of God's grace. When God calls, who are we to defy? Jesus called Paul to be an apostle to the Gentiles, and never once would he dare question either the source of that calling or its responsibility. While there were some, particularly in the Corinthian church, who questioned the authenticity of Paul's apostleship, the apostle himself vigorously defended his authority. His call on the way to Damascus was as real as the call to Peter, James, and John by the Sea of Galilee or as the call to Matthew by the tax booth. It was to this call, initiated by God's grace and purpose, that the apostle gave all credit for his successful mission endeavors throughout the Roman Empire. But the call itself is not something he sought or something men bestowed upon him: he was convinced that his apostleship was "not from men nor through man, but through Jesus Christ and God the Father who raised Him from the dead" (Gal. 1:1).

When God calls a person, the response can be only yes or no. He wants absolute acceptance. No half-minded response will do. Abraham in Ur, Moses by the burning bush, Gideon by the threshing floor, Esther in a strange land, Peter while fishing, Paul on the way to Damascus—each had their call. From the moment of his call, Paul considered himself not only an apostle to the Gentiles but a "bondservant of Jesus Christ" (Rom. 1:1).

The Recipients

Paul uses three descriptive words to identify the recipients of his Epistle: "to the saints who are in Ephesus, and faithful in Christ Jesus" (Eph.1:1).

First, the word "saints." Paul uses the word quite frequently in his Epistles. Of the 60-plus times the word is used in the New Testament, more than 40 are Pauline. Church history and tradition have created an aura around the word "saint," as though it denotes an elite, super-holy few within the church. The Roman Catholic Church has created an entire ecclesiastic procedure whereby a person can be pronounced a saint—only after the individual's death and after the church has completed a checklist of that person's life activities, verifying the holiness of ministry, miracles performed, and ability to listen to and translate ordinary people's prayers to God and successfully initiate answers. But the biblical concept of a saint knows no such beatification procedure.

The most commonly used New Testament word for saint is *hagios,* meaning set apart to be "faithful in Christ Jesus" (verse 1; see Rev. 14:12). Saintship has nothing to do with moral perfection. Nor is it a result of personal character. The key definition of a saint is a sinner saved by Jesus Christ. A saint is not necessarily a good person but a person who by faith has experienced the goodness of God. No permanency of status is attached to the word, but only the possibility that as long as one remains in Christ that person is one of God's saints.

The second descriptive phrase Paul uses is "[those] who are in Ephesus." The early church almost universally accepted that the Epistle was addressed to the saints in Ephesus, but some important ancient manuscripts omit the phrase "in Ephesus," and hence the problem of whether the Epistle was really written to Ephesians. Conservative scholarship generally accepts Ephesus as the destination of the Epistle, but the Epistle perhaps was intended as an encyclical to be circulated in surrounding churches as well. Since the Epistle does not deal with any particular theological or ethical problem, the apostle may have taken the time to portray something he had not done in other Epistles—to place Christ's work in a cosmic perspective, and to show to the entire world and coming generations that Jesus Christ is the Lord of the cosmos.

What better place to show this than in Ephesus, a city that believed that Diana leaped down from Jupiter and hence deserved all worship and praise! In contrast to that false system, Paul wants to show the Ephesians—and through them the entire Christian world—that Jesus Christ did not jump from any planet but came from His Father's abode, "the heavenly places" (Eph. 1:3), in order to unite "together in one all things in Christ, both which are in heaven and which are on earth" (verse 10).

The Epistle's destination is thus the "saints who are in Ephesus."

The third descriptive phrase is "faithful in Christ Jesus." A saint is a Christian with two addresses. One is a spot on earth (here, Ephesus), which is temporary, and the other is "in Christ," which is permanent. The first one may change from time to time, but the second one must never change, for it is fidelity to the second that defines our status as saints.

What makes a Christian faithful? Is it because he or she is an honest person, a good person, or a nice person in relating to others? A Christian must be all that and more. One cannot be a Christian without an anchor of faith, firm and unshakable. That faith must first of all be in the person and work of Jesus Christ. Without belief in the cross and the resurrection of Christ, how can one be a faithful saint? Without total surrender to the claims of Christ, to live like Him, to speak like Him, to walk like Him, to relate like Him, how can one be faithful to Him?

This necessity for absolute loyalty to Christ needs to be emphasized, for we live in a world where too many take the name of Christ in vain. We have "rice Christians," who take up that precious name for some economic advantage. We have "ladder Christians," who find in the embracing of the church a social upward mobility. We have "sprinkled Christians"—sprinkled with water at baptism, with confetti at marriage, and with dust at death. To such, Christianity means something only at those times when they are hatched, matched, and dispatched. Against all this, the Christ of the cross bids the believing, the faithful, and the trusting to come and abide in Him.

Paul's Invocation on the Saints

What is the benefit of being faithful saints in Christ? Paul provides a brief answer to this question before he goes into the Epistle proper: "Grace to you and peace from God our Father and the Lord Jesus Christ" (verse 2). Both grace and peace are customary Pauline greetings in most of his Epistles (Rom. 1:7; 1 Cor. 1:3; 2 Cor. 1:2; Gal. 1:3; etc.). Instead of the traditional Greek word for grace, *chairein,* a form of greeting wishing one health and prosperity (Acts 23:26), Paul uses *charis,* a word that was beginning to acquire a new meaning in the Christian faith. Grace is God's unmerited favor toward sinners, by which He provides us salvation from sin. It is that joy of salvation, that exuberance that comes as a result of belonging to a redeemed family, that lies at the foundation of all Christian greetings and relationships.

Paul adds "peace" in his greetings to his readers. The "peace" that Paul wishes is a result of a new relationship that Christ establishes between believers and God through redemption from sin. The death and resurrection of Christ brought peace between God and sinners, and healed the broken relationships among human beings. With sin's dominion overthrown on the cross, we have peace both vertically and horizontally (Rom. 5:1).

The Christian concept of peace does not depend on external comfort or circumstances. It deals with the internal and the relational. It hits at the core problem of sin. Am I at peace with God? That's the first question. The second follows naturally—am I at peace with my neighbor?

Hence, Paul sources both grace and peace in "God our Father and the Lord Jesus Christ" (Eph. 1:2). "Father" was Jesus' favorite way of referring to God. But what kind of God? A nameless mighty force? The first principle, of which Greek philosophy was so proud? The supreme and measureless Mind that Hindus talk about? Someone who sits up in the clouds caring not a whit as to what happens here on earth? A supercop, who keeps an eye on law and order down below? A stern judge, who tries to perform the tricky art of balancing the good and the evil? An indulgent grandpa, with a bagful of goodies to be thrown down at his will?

The word "Father" at once strikes down these and other immature concepts of God. Instead, God is the "Father of our Lord Jesus Christ." Paul wants us to keep clear that link between the Father and Jesus. This God is real, personal, caring, and approachable.

The fatherhood of God immediately offers to us the concept of true love. God's love has not only created us but has sought out to redeem us from sin. In describing God's love, the New Testament uses the word *agape,* a sacrificial, outgoing, unmerited love. It neither changes nor oscillates; it is utterly dependable. It is love for love's own sake. It loves us, not because we deserve it, but because we are in need of it. This love has placed the utmost dignity on human life—if there were only one sinner, Christ would have died for that single prodigal. That's another reason that Paul wants us to appreciate God as our Father and the Father of the Lord Jesus Christ.

The Dominant Themes

As noted, the book of Ephesians deals with no particular problem in that church. Instead, the apostle ponders over what "God our Father and the Lord Jesus Christ" have done for humanity. In so positioning God and Christ as one in the purpose of saving humanity from sin and in restoring a reconciled creation, Paul underscores the equality of the Father and the Son. The divinity of Christ is not to be debated. He is God, and so is coequal and coeternal with the Father. But He is also Jesus, one who was born in Bethlehem, grew up in Nazareth, walked and ministered on earth, and finally was crucified and rose again.

Christ the divine one and Jesus in human flesh are one and the same person—the second in the Godhead. Christianity exists on the two pillars of the divinity and humanity of Christ. Neither can be taken away without doing away with Christian revelation. As God, Christ is the embodiment and manifestation of both the grace and the love of the Godhead toward humanity. As man He succeeded where Adam failed. He defeated Satan and accomplished the redemptive purposes of the Godhead. Hence the focus of the Epistle is on what God has done *in Christ.*

"In Christ" is one of the predominant themes of the Epistle, and is introduced right at the outset (Eph. 1:3). The phrase and its variations ("in Him," "in whom," etc.) appear some 200 times in Paul's writings, 30 of which are in Ephesians. It is the apostle's favorite way of affirming that whatever God has made possible for the new humanity was accomplished in, and only in, Christ.

Without the incarnation, death, and resurrection of Jesus, humanity would have been left helpless, a prey to Satan and his vile schemes. It is in and through Christ that God's eternal purposes in Creation, history, redemption, and restoration have been fulfilled. Christ is the key to everything we have from God, and it is He who made it possible for us to address God as our Father and to come "boldly to the throne of grace, that we may obtain mercy and find grace to help in time of need" (Heb. 4:16). Thus in every way the Epistle is a Christ-centered letter; it is a hymn of praise and thanksgiving to Christ.

A second theme of the Epistle is redemption and restoration. This is nothing strange to Paul, who saw in the gospel of Jesus Christ "the power of God for salvation to everyone who believes. . . . For in it the righteousness of God is revealed from faith to faith" (Rom. 1:16, 17).

The community of faith in Christ is a redeemed community, redeemed from sin and restored unto righteousness. Further, such a redeemed community does not stand alone; it stands as a community reconciled unto God through Jesus Christ (2 Cor. 5:16-18). The apostle sketches this provision of God for reconciliation and restoration from its very inception in the mind of God "before the foundation of the world" (Eph. 1:4) to its ultimate gathering in the eschatological "fullness of the time" (verse 10).

From the accomplishment of divine-human reconciliation, the Epistle moves to a third important theme: unity. The book of Ephesians posits ultimate unity in the universe in the mind and will of God. All things move in accordance with "His good pleasure which He purposed in Himself" (verse 9).

No one understood this better than Paul. He knew the nature and the cause of human divisiveness. He had been a devout Jew, a member of the Sanhedrin, and a Pharisee of the Pharisees; he had firmly believed that Israel was a chosen race. Like most Jews of his time, he knew and practiced the line of division that separated the Jew from the Gentile. As a Roman citizen, he knew the wall that separated the Romans from the barbarians. As a person well versed in Greek philosophy, he knew the line that defined the free and the slave. Division among human beings was nothing new to Paul.

But when Jesus of Nazareth confronted Paul on his way to Damascus, two of the most important revelations he received were that Jesus Christ is God's way of redemption from sin and that this new world of redemption has neither frontiers nor walls. He accepted the call to be an apostle to the Gentiles seriously and unreservedly, and it totally affected his life and ministry.

He was perhaps the first of the disciples to grasp the enormity of this truth. As an associate of Barnabas, he was an eyewitness to how the walls of separation came tumbling down in the church at Antioch. He saw how both Jews and Gentiles, men and women, Romans and barbarians, became members of one great family of God—all received the Holy Spirit (Acts 11:20-30). With such an experience, Paul told the Galatians: "For you are all sons of God through faith in Christ Jesus. For as many of you as were baptized into Christ have put on Christ. There is neither Jew nor Greek, there is neither slave nor free, there is neither male nor female; for you are all one in Christ Jesus" (Gal. 3:26-28).

In Ephesians Paul speaks of two kinds of unity. First, there is the unity of believers in Christ. The apostle was writing to a multiethnic church. Among its members were Jews and Gentiles, Asiatics and Europeans, slaves and freemen—all visible symbols of a divided humanity. Perhaps most predominant was the wall between Jews and Gentiles. That wall permitted no social contact between the two groups, but insisted on the superiority of one over the other.

Paul devotes the entire second chapter of Ephesians to explaining how Christ's death on the cross broke down that wall, and how the new order He established made circumcision null and void.

The truth of this new unity that Christ brought about between Jews and Gentiles was something that could not have had its origin or its understanding in human design. The truth is God's and was fulfilled by God, who through Jesus on the cross abolished the law of circumcision that divided humanity and created "one new man from the two, thus making peace" (Eph. 2:15). Paul calls this "the mystery" (Eph. 3:3). Unity of believers—across the divisions of language, nationality, race, gender, or whatever—is an act of God, and stands as a core theme of the Epistle.

The second aspect of this doctrine of unity that Paul reveals in Ephesians is cosmic in dimension. Sin has not only brought about division between people, but has disrupted the harmony and unity that existed in the created order before the entrance of sin. Nature itself is a witness to this cosmic hatred and division. The animosity between species, raging volcanoes, destructive earthquakes and tornadoes, the sadness that must have marked the unfallen worlds at the course our earth has taken—all these cry out for the day of liberation when all disharmony will give way to the unity that will prevail when God will "gather together in one all things in Christ, both which are in heaven and which are on earth—in Him" (Eph. 1:10). As William Barclay comments: "The central thought of Ephesians is the realization of the disunity in the universe and the conviction that it can become unity only when everything is united in Christ."[1]

From unity Paul moves on to stress another cosmic theme: "For we do not wrestle against flesh and blood, but against principalities, against powers, against the rulers of the darkness of this age, against spiritual hosts of wickedness in the heavenly places" (Eph. 6:12). The reality of the Christian warfare, as part of the great controversy between Christ and Satan, weighs heavily on the apostle's mind. Its reality and its dangers grip him, and he sees that warfare as affecting every arena of a believer's life—in personal living, at home, at work, at worship—and the apostle warns the Christian to be aware of its dangers.

Thus Christian life, both in its theological grounding and its practical application, occupies the apostle's joys and concerns in this glorious Epistle, which some have called the "'Alps of all the New Testament'. . . in the midst of peaks—Paul's nine epistles written to seven churches."[2]

---

[1] William Barclay, *The Letters to the Galatians and the Ephesians* (Edinburgh: Saint Andrew Press, 1976), p. 66.

[2] *The Seventh-day Adventist Bible Commentary,* vol. 6, p. 995.

CHAPTER 3

Praise and Prayer

Ephesians 1:3-14

After the introductory greetings, Paul begins the Epistle to the church at Ephesus with a long prayer. The prayer consists of two parts: first, one of praise and thanksgiving (Eph. 1:3-14), and second, a prayer for the church at Ephesus (verses 15-23). Christian life must always begin with praise to God and then move on to prayer for ourselves and others. The order is important. God must always come first. An acknowledgment of His role in our lives—our need of Him—must ever inform the spiritual arena of our existence.

Often we make the mistake of rushing to God's throne and placing our petty requests there without recognizing His awesome presence. It is true that the Holy Spirit can sift our prayers and present them in just the right manner that is pleasing to God, but it is important to develop a spiritual maturity that recognizes God's priority in our prayer life.

Paul's hymn of thanksgiving and praise (verses 3-14) is one long sentence in Greek, without any break. It is as though the Holy Spirit had taken hold of the apostle and guided his hands word after word, phrase after phrase, thought after thought, to describe the indescribable—what God has done for sinful human beings through His Son, Jesus Christ.

To begin with, Paul's doxology is Trinitarian in structure. For a Jewish scholar to speak of the Father, Son, and the Holy Spirit is unthinkable. No Jew would ever concede that the Bible that presents the oneness of God also reveals the Trinitarian nature of the Godhead. But Paul's conversion was so total that his transition from Judaism to Christianity included both his understanding of God and his salvation experience—the biblical revelation of God in the three persons of the Father, the Son, and the Holy Spirit, and the glorious truth that salvation is a free gift of God's grace.

In the opening verses of Ephesians the Trinitarian structure emerges clearly. Paul presents the entire Godhead as involved in the formation of the church. God the Father "chose us in Him [in Christ] before the foundation of the world" (verse 4). It is in Christ that "we have redemption through His blood" (verse 7), and through Him the eternal purposes of God are fulfilled (verses 10, 11). The Holy Spirit provides us security and guarantees our eternal inheritance (verses 13, 14).

While recognizing that God is at work here on earth and here in history, the apostle never loses sight of the transcendence of God. God's immanence (that is, His work on earth and His immediacy to us) is important for Paul, but not at the cost of His transcendence (that is, His presence in the "heavenly places" and His role as the sovereign of the cosmos).

Likewise, the humanity of Jesus is important for our salvation experience, but we can ill afford to forget or be indifferent to His divinity. The "here" and "the entirely other" are aspects of biblical theology that ever remind us that the God who reigns in heaven is also the one who taps on our shoulders, walks with us, and wants to dwell in our hearts. Heaven is His throne, but earth is His footstool (Isa. 66:1).

Spiritual Blessings From "Heavenly Places" (Ephesians 1:3)

Paul uses the phrase "in heavenly places" four times in Ephesians. What does this phrase mean? First, it is where our blessings come from (Eph. 1:3). God is the source and means of all blessings, spiritual and material. Here Paul praises God in a special way for the spiritual blessings that come from heavenly places. Spiritual blessings are the ones that are mediated through the Holy Spirit, and they have to do with the inner person. Are we discouraged? Does a particular sin seem to be insurmountable? Are our relations with others incompatible with our Christian beliefs? Is our marriage on the rocks? No amount of money can solve these problems. No stock options can remedy the infractions in our inmost self. But the Spirit can and will.

Second, it is in heavenly places that the risen Lord is seated (Eph. 2:6) to perform His intercessory work on our behalf. Christ is our mediator with the Father. What greater blessing can Christians expect than to have the Lord Himself intercede on their behalf? "The risen Christ, who is now set down on the throne at the right hand of the Father, is the Mighty Healer. . . . Through Him alone can sinners come to God just as they are."[1]

Third, heavenly places indicate God's abode where Christ is seated, where we too will be seated. To what heights has God planned to lift those who are redeemed through Christ! The redeemed will ever be a specially privileged creation in the new heaven and the new earth, for God Himself shall dwell with them, and they with Him (Rev. 21:1-3).

Fourth, it will be in "the heavenly places" that the church will have an opportunity to share with angels their experience of what God has done to redeem them from sin.

Finally, the church will have all the above privileges only as it steadfastly fights "against spiritual hosts of wickedness" and wins the war that had its origin "in heavenly places" (Eph. 6:12, KJV). The church does not stand alone in this warfare. Through His death on the cross Christ has crushed the demonic forces, won the crucial victory over sin and Satan, and offers that victory to the believers. All we need to do is accept His free offer, made possible by God's eternal purpose (Eph. 3:11).

Having described the spiritual blessings that flow from heavenly places, Paul turns to praise God for the unspeakable riches He has endowed upon the believers. At times Paul seems to be at a loss for words, while at other times he soars into heights of ecstasy and joy. But the apostle never loses sight of the big picture he wants to paint before the saints of Ephesus and us: the greatness of God and the majesty of His love toward unworthy sinners such as we.

In Christ He Chose Us (Ephesians 1:4)

Paul's praise and thanksgiving begins where every believer's day must begin and end—in acknowledgment that God is the reason for our status as members of His family. He "blessed us" (Eph. 1:3), "chose us" (verse 4), "predestined us to adoption as sons" (verse 5), "made us accepted" (verse 6), made His "grace" "to abound toward us" (verses 7, 8), "made known to us the mystery" (verse 9), and called us instruments of "praise of His glory" (verse 12).

God's initiative to choose is neither accidental nor an afterthought, but was conceived in His mind even "before the foundation of the world" (verse 4). "The words suggest that the salvation of men through Christ is *prior* to the physical creation and the historical process, not an afterthought of the Creator or an accident of evolution; the universe was brought into being as a theater wherein God might manifest his power and his love in the development of beings fit to sing his praise—holy and blameless."[2]

After saying "[God] chose us in Him" (verse 4), Paul states that God's election expects us to "be holy and without blame before Him in love." Just because God has elected us is no guarantee that we will not fall from that election. Judas was chosen, but he fell. Israel was elected as a special race, but they failed to reach their potential. Hence Peter's warning: "Therefore, brethren, be even more diligent to make your call and election sure, for if you do these things you will never stumble" (2 Peter 1:10). The doctrine of election points to a privilege and requires a life in accordance with God's character. It does not provide the "luxury" of "once saved, always saved."

Yet how many Christians have fallen victim to this dangerous doctrine! Nowhere does the Bible teach such a false assumption. Indeed, it is Satan's cunning ploy to lead Christians to take the salvation experience for granted, and to lead a life of lethargy and indifference. Once saved does not mean always saved. Otherwise, why would the Scriptures warn us to be watchful and stand firm (1 Cor. 16:13), to "not submit again to a yoke of slavery" (Gal. 5:1, RSV), to "put on the whole armor of God, that you may be able to stand against the wiles of the devil" (Eph. 6:11), and to "be the more zealous to confirm your call and election" (2 Peter 1:10, RSV)?

Predestination and Adoption (Ephesians 1:5, 6)

Paul's discussion of God choosing us through Christ is immediately followed by a passage that has been the subject of much debate in church history: "Having predestined us to adoption as sons by Jesus Christ to Himself, according to the good pleasure of His will, to the praise of the glory of His grace, by which He has made us accepted in the Beloved" (Eph. 1:5, 6).

The word "predestination" has given rise to the false notion that in some arbitrary fashion God has already decided who should be saved and who should be lost. But such a teaching violates two of the cardinal truths of the Bible: (1) God's provision for salvation is for all who believe (John 3:16); (2) God has given the power of choice to all humans, so that each person's destiny, from Adam on, is in his or her own hands. God does not interfere with the free exercise of choice to accept or reject His provision (Eze. 18:31, 32; 33:11; 2 Peter 3:9).

What, then, was predestined? Simply this—all those in Christ will be saved. Salvation and eternal life are predestined to be available to all as a free gift of God in Jesus (John 3:16; Eph. 2:8, 9), but only "whoever believes in Him" shall be saved. The universal nature of the gift is predestined; the contingent nature of that gift is determined by human choice. The perimeter of that gift—"in Christ"—is predetermined; that is to say, salvation is available within the circle of being "in Christ." God had drawn this circle of salvation—in Christ—before the foundation of the world. Who comes and stays within the circle is left to individual choice.

Predestined for what? The apostle adds a word that would have carried a lovely meaning for his readers, and so it should to us as well. God,

Paul says, has chosen and predestined us to be "[adopted] as sons by Jesus Christ to Himself, according to the good pleasure of His will" (Eph. 1:5).

During Paul's time Roman law provided for adoption, and those who were adopted as sons and daughters had all the privileges that one's own children enjoyed, including inheritance and citizenship. Indeed, under this law it was not uncommon for some families to adopt their slaves, giving them freedom, inheritance, and citizenship. The apostle possibly had this picture in mind when he wrote to those who are held captive to sin by Satan. When such men and women accept Jesus they become full partners in the family of God. Theirs is freedom from sin. Theirs is inheritance of every promise that God has made. Theirs is citizenship in heaven.

Forgiveness and Redemption (Ephesians 1:7, 8)

Adoption into God's family makes us part of God's family. We are no longer orphans, nor are we prodigals. What made us orphans and prodigals is our choice to leave home for the distant land of sinful life; we became rebels, separated from the heavenly Father. Scripture graphically portrays our sinful status: "Your iniquities have separated you from your God; and your sins have hidden His face from you, so that He will not hear" (Isa. 59:2).

From sin God redeems us, brings us home, and adopts us as His children. Our sins are forgiven and cast "into the depths of the sea" (Micah 7:19). But on what basis was this forgiveness and redemption accomplished? Paul's answer is unequivocal: "In Him we have redemption through His blood, the forgiveness of sins, according to the riches of His grace" (Eph. 1:7). The statement makes clear three points about redemption and forgiveness.

First, redemption and forgiveness are possible only in Christ. Whether one likes it or not, one must face the fact that apart from Christ there is no provision for redemption. Some may call such a statement one of arrogance or bigotry or both. In Paul's time the Greeks called it foolishness and the Jews found it a stumbling block (1 Cor. 1:23). But those who believed found it to be God's power unto salvation (verse 30).

When it comes to sin, the fundamental issue is that we are helpless. We cannot earn salvation through our own merits of good work. Sin is not a health problem, an occupational hazard, an environmental delusion, or even a moral failure. It is basically a rebellion against God, and only God can provide a solution to the problem. He has done that in Christ.

Second, redemption and forgiveness are possible only "through His blood." The biblical doctrine of forgiveness of sin is based on the nonnegotiable principle "Without shedding of blood there is no remission" of sin (Heb. 9:22). John the Baptist recognized Christ for who He was: "The Lamb of God who takes away the sin of the world!" (John 1:29). Christ Himself was conscious of His life being offered as a ransom for the redemption of sinners: "The Son of Man did not come to be served, but to serve, and to give His life a ransom for many" (Mark 10:45). Peter spoke plainly: "You were not redeemed with corruptible things, like silver or gold, . . . but with the precious blood of Christ" (1 Peter 1:18, 19).

What is laid out in these and other verses is the simple truth that we are not saved by Jesus the good man, or Jesus the master teacher, or Jesus the perfect example. We are saved by the death of Jesus. He died for our sins. He died in our stead (Rom. 5:6-8). Lest we forget that, Jesus asserted at the Last Supper that His blood was to be "shed for many for the remission of sins" (Matt. 26:28).

That shedding of blood is crucial for the experience and appreciation of salvation. For one thing, it speaks about sin. Sin is real. Sin is costly. Sin's grip is so intense and deadly that forgiveness of sin and freedom from its power and guilt are impossible without the shedding of the "precious blood of Christ" (1 Peter 1:19). This truth about sin needs to be said again and again because we live in a world that denies the reality of sin or remains indifferent to it. Vivekananda, a Hindu philosopher, once said that "it is a sin to call a man a sinner. It is a standing libel on human nature."[3]

That may well be the view of many today—from the materialist who defines life's occupation in terms of possession to the philosophic humanist who captures life's pursuit in terms of self-fulfillment. But not at the cross. There we are confronted with the diabolical nature of sin, which can be crushed only by that blood "poured out for many for the forgiveness of sins" (Matt. 26:28, NIV).

Let us never forget or be indifferent to the fact that Jesus died for our sins. Without His death there could be no forgiveness. It is our sins that drove Jesus to the cross. As Ellen White states, sin "weighed heavily upon Christ, and the sense of God's wrath against sin was crushing out His life."[4] "Christ was treated as we deserve, that we might be treated as He deserves. He was condemned for our sins, in which He had no share, that we might be justified by His righteousness, in which we had no share. He suffered the death which was ours, that we might receive the life which was His. 'With His stripes we are healed.'"[5]

Third, redemption and forgiveness come "according to the

riches of His grace" (Eph. 1:7). Paul uses the word "riches" six times in this Epistle (1:7, 18; 2:4, 7; 3:8, 16). We may be poor and destitute in many ways, but we are bountiful and rich in God's grace. What good are this world's riches if we have not received God's grace? Grace is a crucial concept in Ephesians. Again and again it appears, underscoring the point that we have nothing to do with either the conception or the execution of the plan of salvation. But for the grace of God we would perish in sin, and our existence itself would have no meaning or purpose.

Mystery of His Will (Ephesians 1:9, 10)

The apostle's prayer of praise moves from individual blessings of election, predestination, adoption, redemption, and forgiveness to a cosmic dimension: "Having made known to us the mystery of His will, according to His good pleasure which He purposed in Himself, that in the dispensation of the fullness of the times He might gather together in one all things in Christ, both which are in heaven and which are on earth—in Him" (Eph. 1:9, 10).

The passage takes us to such spiritual heights that only those who have experienced the blessings Paul had mentioned earlier can fully grasp the significance of what he is now saying. He places the event of the cross and the redemptive activity of God in a cosmic perspective, and returns to this theme again and again. To Paul, sin has ruptured a harmony that once existed in the universe, and unless that rupture is completely eradicated, God's eternal purposes will not reach their victorious fulfillment. He calls this process God's "[gathering] together in one all things in Christ, both which are in heaven and which are on earth" (verse 10).

The depth of Paul's understanding is amazing, and it is evident in the terms he uses. He calls the process a "mystery," and he uses the word several times (1:9; 3:3, 4, 9; 6:19) to underline its divine nature. What is this mystery?

The Greek word *musterion* in classical usage referred to " 'anything hidden or secret,' and it was used . . . to refer to the sacred rites of the Greek mystery religions in which only the initiated shared. [However, in New Testament usage the word] signifies a secret which is being, or even has been, revealed, which is also divine in scope, and needs to be made known by God to men through His Spirit."[6]

To Paul, both the content and the purpose of this mystery are incomprehensible to the human mind without divine revelation (see Gal. 1:11, 12). Paul sought "to show that it was through a special manifestation of divine power that he had been led to see and grasp the great truths of the gospel. It was through instruction received from God Himself that Paul was led to warn and admonish . . . in so solemn and positive a manner."[7]

Thus, mystery, in the Pauline sense, is not something hidden and secretive, or something that is impossible to understand. It is something that was not understood in the past but now has been revealed. Still, it may remain a mystery to those who refuse to accept that revelation.

Now, what is this mystery that Paul is speaking about? Ephesians 3 identifies one part of this mystery as God's plan to bring Jews and Gentiles into one fellowship, to create one new community—a church without walls. But this is only a foretaste of something greater that God has "purposed in Himself, that in the dispensation of the fullness of the times He might gather together in one all things in Christ, both which are in heaven and which are on earth—in Him" (Eph. 1:9, 10).

Paul argues that this mystery of "[gathering] together in one all things" will be accomplished "in the dispensation of the fullness of the times." Just as "in the fullness of the time" God sent His Son to make known the mystery of salvation (Gal. 4:4), so in the fullness of time at the close of this age, God will restore universal harmony in heaven and on earth.

"In the dispensation of the fullness of the time" carries a significant meaning to the Christian concept of history. The Greek word for "dispensation" is *oikonomia,* which is also translated "plan" (RSV) or "administration" (NASB). God has an administrative plan for this universe. History is in the hand of God. He plans, administers, arranges, handles, and prepares all things toward the climactic consummation "in Christ" at the end of this age when Christ shall return the second time.

This is why the cyclic concept of history with its inherent meaninglessness is alien to the biblical worldview. The Bible looks at history as linear, meaningful, purposive, and directional. It moves inexorably toward its finale. From Creation to restoration God's purpose dominates history, testifying that God is the God of history; history is His work.

Hence Christ's passion, crucifixion, resurrection, ascension, and second coming are positive signposts of the Christian view of history. That history marches to its culmination in the administrative plan of God as He wraps up His eternal purposes "in Him" (Eph. 1:10)—that is, in Christ's second coming. That's when God will "gather together in one all things in Christ, both which are in heaven and which are on earth."

Some see in this statement a universal salvation—that is to say, no one will be lost; everyone will be saved. Nothing can be further from truth.

The consummative focus of biblical history is the return of Christ, who will confront the present age and all that it represents. The One who brought the good news of grace will stand at the last day as the pronouncer of judgment on a fallen and rebellious order. The climactic moment in the history between good and evil will witness the unleashing of divine wrath against every expression of hostility and rebellion toward God. That is the moment when sin and sinners and their archleader, Satan (2 Peter 3:10-13), will be purged.

Divine harmony will be restored in heaven and on earth; all things will be placed under the headship of Christ, and "one pulse of harmony and gladness [will beat] through the vast creation."[8] This administrative plan of God toward universal unity and oneness, Paul asserts, is "the mystery of His will, according to His good pleasure" (Eph. 1:9).

Inheritance (Ephesians 1:11, 12)

Paul further adds that believers "have obtained an inheritance being predestined according to the purpose of Him who works all things according to the counsel of His will" (verses 11). *The New English Bible* translates it this way: "In Christ . . . we have been given our share in the heritage." While the Old Testament applied the word "inheritance" to Israel (Ps. 33:12; see also 1 Kings 8:51; Ps. 106:40, etc.), Paul applies it to all those who believed "in Christ." In Christ, both Jews and Gentiles have become God's saints (Eph. 1:1), God's inheritance (verse 14), and God's "possession" (verse 14).

That this should be so is "according to the good pleasure of His will" (verse 5), and who shall question the sovereignty of His purpose? Hence Paul's emphasis is that Jews and Gentiles become one people and one heritage of one God and one Lord.

This purpose of God had two aspects: one is God's, which He has accomplished through Christ; the other is ours, which includes trust in Christ, hearing and accepting the word of truth, and believing in the gospel of salvation (verse 13). So our inheritance is not automatic but conditional on our relationship with and to what God has done through Jesus Christ. When we accept Christ and abide in Him, we enjoy eternal life (1 John 5:11-13), and we become "heirs of God and joint heirs with Christ" (Rom. 8:17).

The Sealing of the Spirit (Ephesians 1:13, 14)

Finally, the apostle concludes the praise portion of his prayer by dwelling briefly on the gift of the Holy Spirit. The Trinitarian picture of

God's salvation once again holds our attention. First, God purposed, predestined, and laid out His administrative plan for our redemption; forgiveness of sins; and the ultimate goal of history, the bringing about of universal harmony. Second, God the Son has accomplished this divine purpose by the shedding of His blood and making the gospel of salvation freely available to all those who receive Him. Third, God the Holy Spirit has sealed and guaranteed the reality of this eternal inheritance.

A seal is a sign of ownership and authenticity. Ranchers put their seal on their cattle to mark their ownership. Documents are sealed to guarantee their authenticity. Likewise, God gives the Holy Spirit to dwell within us as a sign that we are His (see Rom. 8:14-17; 2 Cor. 1:22). We belong to Him; we are not our own (1 Cor. 6:19).

Further, the Epistle calls the Spirit God's guarantee that what He began in Jesus Christ, He will complete in us. The Greek word for "guarantee" can also be translated "deposit," "pledge," an "initial payment." Through the Spirit God has made a deposit, a pledge, that He will fulfill all His promises to both Jews and Gentiles alike "unto the praise of his glory" (Eph. 1:14). What's more, we can enjoy the gifts and the fruit of the Spirit right now (Eph. 4:7-13; Gal. 5:22, 23). Our privilege now is an initial foretaste of the unspeakable riches that God has in store in the fullness of His eternal plan.

Thus ends Paul's prayer of praise. Several times in this passage (Eph. 1:3-14) Paul describes how we become God's people—according to His purpose. Three times he tells us why we became God's people—to the praise of God's glory. The *how* is our call; the *why* is our duty.

---

[1] Ellen G. White, *Mind, Character, and Personality* (Nashville: Southern Pub. Assn., 1977), vol. 2, p. 706.

[2] *The Interpreter's Bible* (Nashville: Abingdon Press, 1981), exegesis on Ephesians 1:4.

[3] Swami Vivekananda, *Speeches and Writings* (Madras: G. A. Natesan, n.d.); quoted in John R. W. Stott, *The Cross of Christ* (Bombay: Gospel Literature Service, 1986), p. 162.

[4] Ellen G. White, *The Desire of Ages* (Mountain View, Calif.: Pacific Press Pub. Assn., 1898), p. 687.

[5] *Ibid.*, p. 25.

[6] *The Illustrated Bible Dictionary* (Wheaton, Ill.: Tyndale, 1980), vol. 2, p. 1041.

[7] White, *The Acts of the Apostles,* p. 386.

[8] Ellen G. White, *The Great Controversy* (Mountain View, Calif.: Pacific Press Pub. Assn., 1911), p. 678.

CHAPTER 4

Prayer for the Church

Ephesians 1:15-23

Except for the first two verses of greetings, Paul devotes the entire first chapter of Ephesians to prayer, leaving us an inspiring example on prayer's role in Christian life and ministry. Prayer unleashes God's power in our lives—power to guide, to comfort, to strengthen, to stand firm, to love the unlovable, to face a Gethsemane, and to hope for the dawn of a new day. A prayerless Christian is a powerless Christian.

Paul's prayer divides itself into two parts, essential in every prayer. In the first part (verses 4-15) the apostle praises God for what He has done for the saints at Ephesus. In the second part (verses 15-23)—again one long sentence in Greek—Paul's focus is threefold: thanksgiving for the quality of the church at Ephesus (verses 15, 16), intercession for that church (verses 17-19), and a jubilant exaltation that the church is the body of Christ (verses 20-23).

Thanksgiving (Ephesians 1:15, 16)

Paul's thanksgiving carries an aura of confidence and authenticity: "Therefore I also, after I heard of your faith in the Lord Jesus and your love for all the saints, do not cease to give thanks for you, making mention of you in my prayers" (Eph. 1:15, 16).

Four distinctive marks characterize Paul's thanksgiving. **First, he is confident that the Ephesians' experience in Christ is real.** The word "therefore" ("for this reason," [NIV]) introduces a causative basis for the apostle's thanksgiving. Paul had sound reason to be thankful for the status of the Ephesian believers—they were recipients of "every spiritual blessing" from heavenly places, already enumerated in verses 3-15. God's selection, predestination, adoption, redemption, forgiveness, unity in Christ, and the sealing of the Spirit are not simply doctrines but heavenly realities that put us on a ceaseless track of thanksgiving. What's more, Paul is thankful that God's grace had enabled the Ephesians to experience the profound mystery of the gospel that brought Jews and Gentiles into one new creation. When history's insurmountable walls came tumbling down, was that not reason enough to thank God for His redemptive power?

Second, Paul says, "after I heard of your faith in the Lord Jesus." This faith must not be taken to mean doctrinal faithfulness, although that is important to one's relationship to the Lord. But here the apostle exults in the trustworthiness and loyalty that the Ephesian church continued to have in Jesus Christ. Believing in Jesus is as essential as trusting in Him and being dependent on Him, and in this the apostle found reason to give thanks to God.

Third, Paul gives thanks to God because the Ephesians possessed the central characteristic of Christian living—"your love for all the saints." Jesus said, "By this all will know that you are My disciples, if you have love for one another" (John 13:35). To the Ephesians, Christianity was more than a system of belief, and faith was more than intellectual assent to a set of doctrines. To them, Christianity was a call to transformed living and dynamic relationship, marked by love to all fellow human beings. However orthodox our doctrines may be, however laudable our worship and witness may be, and however faithful our stewardship may be, we cannot be Christians until we are marked by a double love—love to God and love to people.

Fourth, Paul's prayer was personal and continuous. "I," says the apostle, "do not cease to give thanks for you, making mention of you in my prayers" (Eph. 1:16). Paul was a true pastor and a genuine evangelist. If we are like him, our prayers will include more of others and less of ourselves. The widow down the street, the homeless, the church elder whose marriage is facing some challenges, the teenager who has dropped out of Sabbath school, the young couple contemplating marriage, and countless others in the daily walk and struggles of life need our prayers. The more involved we are in praying for others, the less time we will have to worry about our aches and pains, our loneliness and our despair.

Faith, love, and prayer go together.

Intercession (Ephesians 1:17-19)

From thanksgiving Paul moves to intercession (verses 17, 18). We are often tempted to make our prayers naive, concentrating on material, self-oriented needs. The greatest antidote for egotism in prayer is intercession. When we pray for one another (James 5:16), we acknowledge that we belong to an interdependent community of faith. It is this interrelatedness of the faith community that makes intercessory prayer so necessary and so powerful. Abraham prayed for Lot, and he was saved from Sodom's destruction (Gen. 18:23-33). Moses prayed, and God stayed His hand from destroying Israel (Ex. 32:32). Mordecai prayed, and God delivered Israel from Haman's planned holocaust (Esther 4:16; 10:3). Jesus prayed that Peter's faith might not fail (Luke 22:32). And Jesus stands today as the great intercessor before the Father for all of us (Rom. 8:34; Heb. 7:25).

"What does intercession comprehend?" asks Ellen White, and answers: "It is the golden chain which binds finite man to the throne of the infinite God. The human agent whom Christ has died to save importunes the throne of God, and his petition is taken up by Jesus who has purchased him with His own blood. Our great High Priest places His righteousness on the side of the sincere suppliant, and the prayer of Christ blends with that of the human petitioner."[1]

Paul's intercessory prayer has one major focus: "That the God of our Lord Jesus Christ, the Father of glory, may give to you the spirit of wisdom and revelation in the knowledge of Him" (Eph. 1:17). Under this major heading of wisdom and knowledge, the apostle lists several important outgrowths that are essential in Christian life.

But what is the wisdom for which Paul prays? He is not speaking of wisdom that is human and natural in origin. To him, wisdom has its origin and definition in God's "revelation," and this revelation is made available by "the God of our Lord Jesus Christ."

Paul's prayer is that God will provide a full revelation of His wisdom to the believers in order that they might know the ultimate goodness of such revelation as opposed to any immediate and fleeting value worldly wisdom may offer.

A second purpose of Paul's prayer for the spirit of wisdom is that they may have "the knowledge of Him." Plato decreed that the first task of a human being is "Know thyself." Paul's decree is "Know your God." The distinction between Plato and Paul is one between life and eternal life, reason and revelation.

There may be nothing wrong with asserting, "Know yourself," but there is the danger that self becomes its own ultimate god, its own final standard. The Pauline formula, "Know your God," opens up the higher vistas of heavenly vision. Under this vision self knows its limitations and is given the opportunity of choosing a radically different life here and in the hereafter. "And this is eternal life, that they may know You, the only true God, and Jesus Christ whom You have sent" (John 17:3).

What does it mean to know God? To Paul, to know God is not mere intellectual knowledge that He exists, that He is the Creator, that He is the sustainer. While all this is true, to Paul the end result of knowledge is not conceptual but experiential. Knowing God is to know Him in a more intimate, personal, experiential way. To know that two parts of hydrogen and one part of oxygen make water is knowledge—true and factual—but such knowledge will not save a person dying of thirst. Unless that water is drunk, unless it becomes part of the human system, mere knowledge of water would remain powerless. So Paul prays that the knowledge of God will move from theory to practice, from mere intellectual acquisition to practical living—affecting the spirit, the mind, the body, the emotions, the relationships of the believer. To know God is to let God control and guide our life at all times.

Another important factor in Paul's prayer about the knowledge of God is his awareness that the soul's eternal enemy never fails in redefining God so as to compromise His true identity. That redefinition may well be Diana in different forms—from a materialistic idol to a philosophic idealism or theological speculation. As a warning against such temptations, Paul prays that the Ephesians may receive the knowledge of the "God of our Lord Jesus Christ" (Eph. 1:17). We cannot separate God and Christ. Christology defines theology. Without the ultimate revelation of God in Christ we could not have the true and fuller knowledge of God. It is that God who revealed Himself in Jesus Christ who should be the object of the Christian's knowledge and life. Seize Jesus. Hang on to Him. Abide in Him. For to know Jesus is to know God, and therein lies eternal life.

But what is the end objective of Paul's prayer "that the God of our Lord Jesus Christ" may give "the spirit of wisdom and revelation in the knowledge of Him" (verse 17)? The apostle's answer is direct and unwavering: "that the eyes of your heart may be enlightened in order that you may know" (verse 18, NIV). While the Greeks considered reason as the core of human personality, the Hebrews viewed the heart as the center of human life and activity. The heart is the seat of human action, purpose, and driving force. It is the center of thought, the anchor of emotions, the source of moral judgment. Both love and judgment, goodness and evil, God's delight and Satan's entrapment, are focused on the human heart. Paul is writing in the Hebrew sense of the word, and his prayer is that the very headquarters of human personality may be transformed and enlightened "by the spirit of wisdom and revelation in the knowledge of Him."

Because of this revelation of wisdom, Christians must be the most enlightened, living with full awareness of four realities: (1) the hope of their calling; (2) the riches and the glory of their inheritance; (3) the manifestation of God's power; and (4) the establishment of the church as His body (verses 18-23).

1. We need to be fully aware of the nature of our calling. That call is a privilege. God has called us to belong to Christ, to be His saints (Rom. 1:6), and to have "fellowship with his Son" (1 Cor. 1:9, NIV), to be liberated from the condemnation of the law (Gal. 5:1, 13), and to enjoy the peace that comes from Christ (Col. 3:15). The call has a responsibility as well. We are to "serve one another in love" (Gal. 5:13, NIV)—maintaining a harmonious and unified relationship with all, cutting across all walls of division; living in "one body" (Col. 3:15); and leading a holy life, worthy of the calling (1 Thess. 4:7; Eph. 4:11)!

2. We need to be aware of the riches and the glory of our inheritance. When the apostle brought the gospel to Ephesus, he was an eyewitness to how the saving power of Jesus Christ disturbed and divided the city. His powerful proclamation of the Word, accompanied by many miracles, brought a spiritual revolution to the city. Their acceptance of the new life in Jesus indeed transformed their lives, and they made a clear break from their past.

Discipleship is a costly affair. Some had to leave their fishing nets. Some had to leave their tax booths. Ephesians had to leave their trade or their shopping centers. But is it worth the cost? Even Peter at one time asked the Lord directly, "See, we have left all and followed You. Therefore what shall we have?" (Matt. 19:27). It is only human that similar questions may have plagued the Ephesians now and then.

Paul prays that God will enlighten the minds of the Ephesian believers that they might see both the riches and the glory of their inheritance that they will receive along with all the saints. Do you consider yourself poor because you have accepted Christ? Have you come down in the social ladder in the eyes of your community? Or is it possible that, because you have embraced the "truth," you have climbed up the ladder of social mobility, as some studies of Adventists indicate? Never mind. In the eyes of God neither our poverty nor our upward mobility counts for anything. Our inheritance is not of this world. In Christ we have "an inheritance incorruptible and undefiled and that does not fade away, reserved in heaven for you, who are kept by the power of God through faith for salvation ready to be revealed in the last time" (1 Peter 1:4, 5).

To look upon this eschatological inheritance as spiritual utopia is to go against every grain of God's promise for His people. Martyn Lloyd-Jones, a great preacher, once said, "I do not hesitate to assert that the more spiritual we are, the more we shall think about heaven. The nearer we are to Christ, the more we shall meditate upon the glory which He has prepared for us. This is an invariable and infallible test of true spirituality."[2]

3. We need to be fully aware of "the exceeding greatness of His power toward us who believe" (Eph. 1:19). This is the first of five times that Paul speaks in Ephesians of the power of God or Jesus Christ at work in our midst, or within us, or for us. The power is exceedingly great—beyond what words can describe. And the power is seen in "us who believe." It is as though Paul is saying, *Look at us. Our life is a testimony of God's power at work. Compare what we were and what we are. Review the darkness of our past and the glorious light of the present. Once we were without hope. Now we have hope. Once we lived in sin. Now we live in righteousness by His grace. How did all this happen? Not by our works. Not by our intelligent designs. We are what we are by the grace and the power of God.* A Christian with Christ's power has no competition. Nothing can stop him or her from reaching the kingdom.

The apostle identifies three mighty deeds that God has accomplished with respect to the gospel. First, it is the power that raised Jesus from the dead (verse 20). Just as God's love at its best was seen in the death of Christ on behalf of sinners (John 3:16; Rom. 5:8), so God's power at its mightiest was seen in Christ's resurrection. This power that brought Christ from the dead is the same power that saves us from sin to salvation. The transformed life is the greatest testimony to the power of the risen Lord, and therefore, Paul could say, Christ in you is "the hope of glory" (Col. 1:27).

Second, God's power exalted Jesus and "seated Him at His right hand in the heavenly places" (Eph. 1:20). The risen Jesus is also the interceding high priest, who stands in the heavenly courts on behalf of those who believe in Him (Heb. 8:1, 2).

Third, God's power has restored all things to Christ. God has placed Christ above "all principality and power and might and dominion, and every name that is named, not only in this age but also in that which is to come. And He put all things under His feet" (Eph. 1:21, 22). Here is the signal to the universe that in the great controversy between Christ and Satan, Christ has won the ultimate victory. He is indeed the Lord of the universe. Lloyd-Jones's comment is significant: "But this applies not only to the material universe, but also the moral universe and the spiritual universe. God has made Him the Head of all; He has given Him this dignity. The Creator of the universe, the Artificer, the Controller of the cosmos, has given to the Son to be in control of everything everywhere."[3]

4. Paul prays for enlightenment that we may be fully aware of the nature of the church as the body of Christ (verses 22, 23).

The Church: The Body of Christ (Ephesians 1:22, 23)

After exploding in glorious words to describe the ascension and exaltation of Jesus (Eph. 1:20-22), the apostle introduces one of the most vivid, expressive, and daring thoughts of the New Testament: the church is the body of Christ, with Himself its head (verses 22, 23).

The body metaphor is rich in what it says about the close relationship between Christ and the church. The vital and intimate relationship that exists between the body and the head is illustrative of the relationship that ought to exist between the church and Christ. Just as all operational control of the body rests in the head, so the life, mission, and purpose of the church rest in Christ. Without Christ, there is no church. He is its builder and maker, and He is the one who will fulfill all of God's promises for the church.

While emphasizing the closeness of relationship between the church and Christ, we must guard against the grave danger of either equating the church with Christ or considering the church as the incarnational extension of Christ. Christ must always be the head of the church, its sovereign Lord and Savior; the church must always remain His body—His to command, His to carry out His will and purpose. Christ is the head of the church; there is no other head. Christ is the authority over the church; there is no other.

While the church as a collective entity is represented in the metaphor of the body, no single individual can assume to be the sole proprietor or representative of that body. "The church is built upon Christ as its foundation; it is to obey Christ as its head. It is not to depend upon man, or be controlled by man. Many claim that a position of trust in the church gives them authority to dictate what other men shall believe and what they shall do. This claim God does not sanction."[4]

Inasmuch as the church is the body of Christ, what is our relationship as church members to Christ? What is our role as pastors and teachers, elders and deacons, parents and children? Where do we stand with reference to Christ in worship and at work, in study and at play, in friendship and stewardship? Being part of the body of Christ is a high privilege and a grave responsibility.

I am reminded of an old story I heard as a boy from my gentle and caring pastor. It's just a story, but it makes a telling point about us as the body of Christ. When Jesus ascended into heaven, He was welcomed by hosts of rejoicing angels with a chorus of victory. As the cosmic chorus ascended in a triumphal crescendo, a great voice announced to all heavenly hosts, "Behold the lamb of God that takes away the sins of the world!"

Just then the angel Gabriel noticed the nail prints on the hands of Christ. In absolute wonder and awe Gabriel exclaimed, "Lord, You must have suffered much to win this victory and to redeem the sinful race."

Jesus answered, "Yes, very much. There was no other way to show how much the Father and I loved erring human beings."

"But do all the people know how much You love them? Do they know that they are saved, free, through the blood You have shed?" asked Gabriel.

"Not all," said Jesus. "Right now, only a few in Jerusalem know."

"But how will the whole world come to know of Your love and grace? And when? And what have You done about it?"

"Well," said Jesus, "I have left that task to a few people—Peter, James, John, and a few others. These will take the good news of salvation to others. Those will tell still others, and so on, until everyone hears that God loves and saves."

"But what if Peter, James, and John give up the task and go back to their nets? Or perhaps those who follow them will forget. Have You made any other plan, just in case?"

"No," said Jesus. "I left no other plan. I told them that I am depending on them. They are My body."

Just a story. But the point is powerful. Jesus has no other hands except ours, no other voice except ours, no other feet except ours to do His work, to sing His praise, to walk His way.

He is counting on His body, the church, to do His task.

---

[1] Ellen G. White, *That I May Know Him* (Washington, D.C.: Review and Herald Pub. Assn., 1964), p. 78.

[2] D. Martyn Lloyd-Jones, *God's Ultimate Purpose: An Exposition of Ephesians 1* (Grand Rapids: Baker Books, 1978), p. 386.

[3] *Ibid.,* p. 439.

[4] White, *The Desire of Ages,* p. 414.

Chapter 5

God's Workmanship

Ephesians 2:1-10

Often called a miniversion of the Epistle to Romans, Ephesians 2:1-10 defines the gospel of Jesus Christ as a powerful and dramatic movement—from death to life, from sin to righteousness, from separation to unity, from aliens to God's workmanship. In this passage Paul introduces the making of God's family in three steps: what we were, what God has done for us, and what we are today.

What We Were (Ephesians 2:1-3)

Most of us are not proud of all our past. We all have something that we wish we could forget. The Bible defines our past condition in one word and our past status in another: sin defines our condition; death our status. We "were dead in trespasses and sins" (Eph. 2:1).

We live in a world that denies sin and laughs at the need of a Savior. A lie is no longer an attempt to deceive but a statement that has become inoperative. A forbidden relationship between a man and a woman is no longer adultery but a behavioral slip that has come to public notice. The manipulation of a corporation to the destruction of its workers is no longer fraud but management failure.

Against such denial syndrome of sin, consider Paul's graphic portrayal of the reality of sin and the finality of its consequence, death. Before we came to Christ, we were all dead in "trespasses and sins." To Paul, sin is so vile and pervasive that it has deprived humanity of the glory bestowed at the time of Creation: "All have sinned and fall short of the glory of God" (Rom. 3:23). "All men, both Jews and Greeks, are under the power of sin. . . . 'None is righteous, no, not one'" (verses 9, 10, RSV). If anyone should dare say that such is not the human predicament, the Bible calls that person a liar (1 John 1:8-10).

If sin is universal in its presence and power, the consequence of sin is no less universal. "The wages of sin is death," says the apostle (Rom. 6:23), and we can be pretty sure that sin is a faithful paymaster. We get what we deserve. Death is our lot, a natural consequence of sin. A life away from God is a life of death. We may be morally upright, do good things, lead respectable lives in the community, but without the commanding presence of Christ in our lives we are spiritually dead. We are insensitive to the prompting of the Holy Spirit. We are deaf to the voice of God. We are blind to His purposes. We ignore His children. We erect walls of separation that divide one person from another, one people group from another. We are dead.

Spiritual death, however, does not mean inactivity. In fact, it is very much a life of activity controlled by Satan, with whom sin began. Paul presents a threefold description of such a life outside of Christ.

First, it is a life in which we "walked according to the course of this world, according to the prince of the power of the air" (Eph. 2:2). When Paul speaks of the "course of this world," he refers to a system that operates outside of the context of God. It's a world that has its own god. It works "according to the prince of the power of the air." That prince is Satan, whom Jesus called "the prince of this world" (John 12:31, NIV). He is "the spirit at work in the hearts of those who refuse to obey God" (Eph. 2:2, NLT). It is under his bondage we lived before we found Christ.

Second, the life outside of Christ is a life of disobedience. Paul describes those who live without Christ as "sons of disobedience" (verse 2). A Christless life seeks its own way, sets its own standards, and makes disobedience to God its hallmark of independence. But in reality there is no freedom in such disobedience. A life that moves away from God is a life that moves closer to Satan, in bondage to the "desires of the flesh and of the mind" (verse 3).

What does Paul mean by "desires of the flesh"? The first thing that comes to mind is sexual sins, but that is just a small part of the story. In his list of the sins of the flesh (Gal. 5:19-21), Paul does begin with adultery and fornication, but goes on to add "uncleanness, lewdness, idolatry, sorcery, hatred, contentions, jealousies, outbursts of wrath, selfish ambitions, dissensions, heresies, envy, murders, drunkenness, revelries, and the like."

While we can take comfort that we do not lead a Christless life, how often do we find such sins as pride, envy, jealousy, revelry, contentions, and divisions among those who claim to be Christ's followers? Wherever we see walls of partition, pleasure without responsibility, discipleship without the cross, worship without fellowship—we see the flesh at work. The "flesh" is a tough enemy to struggle with, and self is our persistent foe. Hence, says Ellen White, "we are commanded to crucify the flesh, with the affections and lusts. How shall we do it? Shall we inflict pain on the body? No; but put to death the temptation to sin. The corrupt thought is to be expelled. Every thought is to be brought into captivity to Jesus Christ. All animal propensities are to be subjected to the higher powers of the soul. The love of God must reign supreme; Christ must occupy an undivided throne."[1]

Third, life outside of Christ is a life lived under the wrath of God. Before they came to Christ, the Ephesians were "by nature children of wrath" (Eph. 2:3). Sin inevitably attracts the wrath of God. God hates sin, but He loves the sinner so much that He gave His only Son to die for that sinner.

God's hatred of sin cannot and must not be transferred to the sinner. That's not the meaning of God's wrath. Wrath is God's righteousness shown in its hostility to sin; His holiness refusing to compromise with the rebellion toward His will; His personal resolve to condemn sin and remove it from the cosmos. Wrath is God's personal attitude of judgment against sin. Before we came to Christ we were in sin and rebellion and under God's judgment and condemnation. But this does not mean that we were denied a way out of that wrath. Indeed, verses 1, 4, and 5 assure us that God Himself has provided a solution to our predicament through Christ, who made us alive.

What God Has Done for Us (Ephesians 2:4-6)

In the face of such a dreadful past, what shall we do? What can a dead person do? Nothing, nothing at all. Try education. It may sharpen our intellectual tools, brighten the horizons of our understanding of nature and its intricacies, and expand the perception of our environment. It even may improve our economic equations. But beyond that, it is powerless to liberate us from sin's bondage. Try humanism. It may help us to live in harmony with others, stress the noble ideals of moral goodness, take us to the height of self-sacrifice for the sake of common good, and even produce a Lincoln or a Gandhi. But beyond that, it subsists only in the denial of sin.

Try psychology. It may help to probe our inner depths, discover our potential for growth, but in the end it must yield to the reality of human depravity. Try anything else—the result will be the cry so dramatically made by Paul's man in bondage: "Who will deliver me from this body of death?" (Rom. 7:24).

Paul also wrote history's daring judgment: "The wages of sin is death" (Rom. 6:23); but the apostle did not continue with what seems a logical corollary to that statement of hopelessness: "The wages of righteousness is life." Had the Holy Spirit inspired him to write that kind of reverse judgment, humanity could pride itself by saying that we can do good and live. For after all, if sin brings death, the opposite of sin must bring the opposite of death. If I earn death because of my sin, I should be able to earn the opposite of death by doing the opposite of sin. Such statements are quite logical. Indeed, whole philosophic and religious systems are built on the foundation that redemption from human depravity can be found within the human.

Not so with Paul. To him, sin is not a lapse in conduct but a rupture in relationship with the Creator, a rebellion against Him, a refusal to be subject to Him (Rom. 8:7). Since rebellion against God involves more than an individualistic mode of existence and takes in the cosmic issues of His love, justice, and holiness, any human attempt to restore that rupture on the basis of human will and power is repugnant to the sovereignty of God. Being dead through trespasses and sins (Eph. 2:1, 5; Col. 2:13), and deserving "to die" (cf. Rom. 1:32), the sinner lives in a state of alienation and hopelessness. The way out of the problem of sin, therefore, cannot lie in the sinner or the sinner's surroundings. What then? Who shall liberate us who are dead in "trespasses and sins"?

Ephesians 2:4-9 provides the answer. The passage begins with two dramatic words: "But God." We were rebels, but God . . . ; we were walking according to the lusts of the flesh, but God . . . ; we were condemned as children of wrath, hopeless and destitute, unable to save ourselves, but God . . . ; we were dead, but God . . . As long as those two words are enshrined in biblical vocabulary we have hope.

God is the only answer to the problem of sin, Satan, and death. He who created life has the power to rescue us from death. "His power is absolute, and it is the pledge of the sure fulfillment of His promises to all who trust in Him. He has means for the removal of every difficulty, that those who serve Him and respect the means He employs may be sustained."[2]

"But God . . ."

"But why?" asks the sinner. Why did God step in to deliver us from the bondage of sin? We deserved to die; why did God choose to save us? Why didn't He leave Adam and Eve to perish in their choice? The apostle provides two answers.

First, because God is "rich in mercy" (Eph. 2:4). Mercy is intrinsic to the character of God. "'The Lord your God is a merciful God,' He will not forsake you nor destroy you" (Deut. 4:31). God's mercy is inexhaustible, and it endures forever (Ps. 103:11). It is this everlasting kindness and compassion of God that made it possible for us to be made alive in Christ.

Second, "because of His great love *[agape]* with which He loved us" (Eph. 2:4). God's everlasting love—selfless on the part of the giver, undeserved on the part of the receiver—is the basis for giving "His only begotten Son, that whoever believes in Him should not perish but have everlasting life" (John 3:16).

Love was God's prime motivation to give His Son to die for us. Paul describes God's gift of His Son as one given to us while we were His enemies (Rom. 5:7, 8). There lies the incredible nature of God's love—love toward the unlovable and the undeserving, love toward the enemy, love that emptied God's heart in order that we may be saved from sin and death.

Paul uses three phrases to explain what God accomplished through Christ, and each phrase in Greek carries the same prefix, *syn,* which means "together with." The prefix has a powerful connotation. What God has done through Christ is the same for all believers, both Greek and Jew. We share the blessings of God's redemptive act together with one another and together with Christ.

"He . . . made us alive together with Christ" (Eph. 2:5). "Made us alive" means simply that He saved us from the death we were in because of our "trespasses and sins." In Christ the spiritually dead are quickened to be spiritually alive.

Then He "raised us up together" (verse 6). Without the resurrection of Jesus, salvation could not have become a reality. Because He lives, we also live. The new life we live is a witness not only to the resurrection power of Christ but also to the new community that will live together. In the final analysis the church is a resurrection family.

Finally, He "made us to sit together in the heavenly places in Christ Jesus" (verse 6). Here is the ultimate fulfillment of God's redemptive plan. Through Christ He not only saved us from sin and raised us from spiritual death; He also offers us the ultimate privilege of sitting with Him in heavenly places at the great eschatological union when all those who are dead in Christ will arise at His second coming to meet Him in the clouds and to begin a life of heavenly togetherness (2 Tim. 2:12; Rev. 22:5).

Note the apostle's emphasis that we shall "sit together." The "we" includes both Jew and Gentile. The great table of heavenly fellowship will make no distinction between people. No color, no race, no language, no gender, no ethnicity will mar that heavenly gathering. That's the good news of restored relationships. But before we can sit together in heaven, must we not taste a little of heaven on earth?

Paul's ecstasy and joy at this threefold accomplishment of God reaches its climax in Ephesians 2:7: "That in the ages to come He might show the exceeding riches of His grace in His kindness toward us in Christ Jesus." What a privilege! The redeemed of the earth will stand as the vindication of God's love and grace. The entire cosmos will testify that God is love—thus countering every accusation Satan has made against God in the great controversy.

God's Grace at Work (Ephesians 2:7-10)

The entire process of how we are saved is summarized in Ephesians 2:8, 9: "For by grace you have been saved through faith, and that not of yourselves; it is the gift of God, not of works, lest anyone should boast." What is the apostle saying? Simply this: God's grace is the basis of our salvation. Our works play no part in it, and we have nothing to boast about. All we need to do is to receive it as a gift through faith in Him. Let's study this in some detail.

By God's grace we are saved. We are familiar with the definition that grace is God's unmerited favor toward us. Grace is the force of love behind God's reaching out to redeem humanity. As sinners we deserve death; God offers us life. We are separated; He offers us reconciliation. We are under judgment; He provides us freedom. We are prodigals in swine land; He brings us home. All for free.

Divine grace is the basis of God's redemptive initiative and operation. When Paul says "the grace of God has appeared for the salvation of all men" (Titus 2:11, RSV), he is not referring to some abstract quality of God but to the dynamic, historic event of Jesus Christ—more specifically, the act of Christ on the cross. That act is God's ultimate revelation of His grace and love toward sinners. That act made possible the forgiveness of sin and the freedom from its bondage. Thus grace is God's initiative and activity for salvation of humanity from sin. There is no other way.

Human works, however good and noble, have nothing to do with the act of divine forgiveness from sin. So far as salvation is concerned, grace and works are mutually exclusive principles. Salvation is by grace through faith alone; there is no such thing as divine grace plus human something. Says the apostle: "For by grace you have been saved through faith; and this is not your own doing, it is the gift of God—not because of works, lest any man should boast" (Eph. 2:8, 9, RSV). The principle is stressed in another way in the Epistle to Romans: "But if it is by grace, it is no longer on the basis of works; otherwise grace would no longer be grace" (Rom. 11:6, RSV).

Paul's message to the Ephesians is in perfect agreement with the teaching of the rest of the Bible. Salvation from sin is a free gift through God's grace. No sin is too great to be forgiven, no person is too far gone. "Whoever comes to me I will never drive away" (John 6:37, NIV) is the divine promise and provision.

David's experience is a good example. After his grievous sins of covetousness, adultery, and murder, David prayed, "Have mercy upon me, O God, according to Your lovingkindness; according to the multitude of Your tender mercies, blot out my transgressions. Wash me thoroughly from my iniquity, and cleanse me from my sin" (Ps. 51:1, 2). David did not plead for God's forgiveness on the basis of the great and good things he had done. He did not ask for salvation because of his meritorious past, of his standing for the name of God and defending that name against all God's enemies. David knew that none of his good works could save him from his sin. So he threw himself contritely at God's feet with the plea "Create in me a clean heart, O God, and renew a steadfast spirit within me" (verse 10).

All are saved as David was—by grace alone. John Newton was leading a life far away from God; he dealt in slavery, denying dignity to thousands of men and women created in God's image. But he came to the point where he found himself helpless and hopeless. When he found forgiveness in the free gift of God's grace, he left to history this famous anthem:

"Amazing grace! how sweet the sound,
That saved a wretch like me!
I once was lost, but now am found,
Was blind, but now I see."

Yes, God's grace is amazing, free, abounding, and ever-assuring. Salvation is the free and unmerited gift of this grace.

But what is the human part? Our part is to believe and accept what God has done through Christ. Paul says: "By grace . . . you are saved, *through faith*" (Eph. 2:8, Phillips). Add to this Jesus' own affirmation: "Whoever believes in Him should not perish but have everlasting life" (John 3:16). As sinners, all we need to do is come in faith to the cross. There we must face the Crucified One and see in Him our substitute. We must acknowledge that He died for our sins (see Rom. 5:8; 14:15; 1 Cor. 15:3; 2 Cor. 5:14). His body was broken for us (see Luke 22:19; 1 Cor. 11:24). His blood was shed for us (see Luke 22:20; 1 Cor. 11:25). When we accept Him as our Savior by faith, His death cancels our death. His life becomes ours. We receive "the free gift of God [which] is eternal life in Jesus Christ our Lord" (Rom. 6:23, RSV).

Here's all we have to do: "Believe on the Lord Jesus Christ, and you will be saved" (Acts 16:31). It's as simple as that. Yet human pride and arrogance insist on salvation by good works. The doctrine of righteousness by works is as old as sin itself. Did not Adam and Eve sew themselves garments of leaves to cover their nakedness and hide themselves from their Creator instead of coming before Him in repentance? Did not Cain choose to murder rather than admit the futility of his own approach to God by the labor of his hands? Did not Abraham and Sarah seek to fulfill the covenant promise through Hagar instead of relying upon God's promise? "The principle that man can save himself by his own works lay at the foundation of every heathen religion. . . . Satan had implanted this principle. Wherever it is held, men have no barrier against sin."[3]

Paul was quite firm in affirming that "we have come to believe in Christ Jesus, so that we might be justified by faith in Christ, and not by doing the works of the law, because no one will be justified by the works of the law" (Gal. 2:16, NRSV). Ellen White writes that the robe of Christ's righteousness, "woven in the loom of heaven, has in it not one thread of human devising."[4]

But to speak of grace as free does not mean that it is not costly. It is free only so far as the recipient is concerned. To the Provider, the price was enormous, the cost inestimable. God's chosen way of dealing with sin through the manifestation of His grace cost the life of His Son. Who can estimate the value of that act of divine love? Gethsemane and the cross show not only divine abhorrence of sin but also the divine cost to effect the plan of salvation. Ephesians 1:7, 8 spells out clearly the price paid: "In him [Christ] we have redemption through his blood, the forgiveness of our trespasses, according to the riches of his grace which he lavished upon us" (RSV). God and His grace, Christ and His blood, our sins and our forgiveness, are all mentioned in this one beautiful passage to show that we have nothing to add to what God has already done. Let all human boastings cease! Let all simply respond in faith and let the blood of Jesus cleanse us from our sins (Rev. 1:5).

After that, what?

What We Are Today (Ephesians 2:9, 10)

Paul's story of salvation does not end in forgiveness only. Paul moves from death to life to God's workmanship. Once we were dead in "trespasses and sins" (Eph. 2:1). Now "we are His workmanship, created in

Christ Jesus for good works, which God prepared beforehand that we should walk in them" (verse 10). Salvation is not self-correction; it is not self-improvement. Salvation is God's creation; indeed, a re-creation, a new creation. Only the Creator can be our Redeemer, and the Redeemer now fashions us into His workmanship—His masterpiece, His exhibit of His grace and love for "ages to come" (verse 7).

Paul adds one more fact of significance: We are made His workmanship "for good works" in order that all may witness that we walk no more according to the world but according to the One who saved us. Salvation is free, but it does not mean freedom from responsibility. Jesus said, "If you love Me, keep My commandments" (John 14:15).

Obedience is not a prerequisite for salvation, but it is a requisite, for "faith without works is dead" (James 2:26). Many Christians view discipleship as the final destination. Discipleship is not an arrival point; it is a journey in process, and the journey can proceed well only if we accept and abide in Christ our Redeemer (John 15:4). Once that constant abiding is established through faith in God's enabling power, fruit follows as a natural course. The principle is a simple one: first grace, then obedience; first love, then its fruit.

Any attempt to deny obedience its role in discipleship makes grace cheap and void. Dietrich Bonhoeffer, a German theologian who ministered against formidable odds during the Nazi rule, coined the term *cheap grace*. "Cheap grace is the preaching of forgiveness without requiring repentance, baptism without church discipline, Communion without confession, absolution without personal confession. Cheap grace is grace without discipleship, grace without the cross, grace without Jesus Christ, living and incarnate."[5]

When Jesus calls a person He gives him or her a cross to carry. As Luther defined, a Christian is a crucian, a person of the cross. To be a disciple is to be His workmanship.

---

[1] Ellen G. White, *The Adventist Home* (Nashville: Southern Pub. Assn., 1952), pp. 127, 128.

[2] Ellen G. White, *The Ministry of Healing* (Mountain View, Calif.: Pacific Press Pub. Assn., 1905), pp. 481, 482.

[3] White, *The Desire of Ages,* pp. 35, 36.

[4] Ellen G. White, *Christ's Object Lessons* (Washington, D.C.: Review and Herald Pub. Assn., 1900), p. 311.

[5] Dietrich Bonhoeffer, *The Cost of Discipleship* (New York: Macmillan Co., 1965), p. 36.

CHAPTER 6

The Church Without Walls

Ephesians 2:11-22

When William Carey arrived in Calcutta, India, in 1793, he soon found a friend in Raj Ram Mohan Roy. The latter was a devout Hindu, but he had disavowed some of the social conventions of Hinduism, such as caste, child marriage, and widow burning. As friends, Carey and Roy had long exchanges on the social stance of their respective religions. Roy was tremendously influenced by the Sermon on the Mount. Together Carey and Roy launched a social reformation that was to impact life in India for years to come.

Carey believed that the power of the gospel can bring about change. Roy believed that the basic goodness in every human being can be challenged to reject social evil and embrace good. The social reformation that the two men launched eventually brought about legislation in India that outlawed child labor, child marriage, and widow burning, and set in motion a historic drive toward the recognition of the basic dignity of all men and women.

However, one thing grieved Ram Mohan Roy much—the inconsistency of Christian faith and practice. There are some who believe that it was this inconsistency that kept many great intellectuals of that time, and even now, from accepting the wonderful truth of the gospel. Once, on a visit to England, Roy was in the home of Thomas Raffles, a pastor in Liverpool. The conversation steered to the subject of brotherhood. The Hindu social activist made a comment that ought to engage every Christian. "You say that you are all one in Christ, all brethren, and equal in Him. . . . Go to the cathedral at Calcutta; there you see a grand chair of crimson, velvet, and gold—that is for the Governor-General. . . . Then there are other chairs of crimson and gold—they are for the members of the [British] council; then there are seats lined with crimson—they are for the [British] merchants. . . . Then there are bare benches for the common people and the poor. . . . If the poor man goes and sits in the chair of the Governor-General, they will break his head! Yet you are all one in Christ!"

What an indictment!

The governor-general is gone. Crimson chairs have disappeared. But the breaking of heads is still around, in one shape or another—even in the Adventist Church. How else can you explain divisions within the church on the basis of caste, color, race, language, economic status, gender (the list goes on)? Is the power of the gospel limited to only the spoken word at church? Must not the power of the gospel break down every wall of prejudice, cut across all human barriers, and be seen and practiced wherever we are—on bended knee, at the workshop, at the Communion table, or in the neighborhood park?

Paul captures the beauty and majesty of Christian unity in Ephesians 2:11-22. He approaches the subject in three steps: "at that time" (verse 12); "but now" (verse 13); "now, therefore" (verse 19).

"At That Time . . . Without Christ" (Ephesians 2:12)

Ephesians 2:11-19 addresses primarily the Gentile Christians at Ephesus. Paul wants them to remember their status before they came to Christ, or rather before Christ found them. Life without Christ and life with Christ stand in absolute contrast with each other, as absolute as darkness and light, death and life. Although the challenge is applicable to all, both Jews and Gentiles, Paul particularly reminds the Gentiles of what they were like before Christ entered their lives so that they would be mindful and rejoice in the privilege of new life in Christ Jesus.

First, Gentiles were subjected to a life of prejudice. They were called "Uncircumcision by what is called the Circumcision" (verse 11). Name-calling at any time or place is offensive to human dignity and to the value that God gives to men and women. Jews called the Gentiles "uncircumcision" in a derogatory sense, and called themselves "circumcision" in a sense of arrogance and self-righteousness. Paul declares the futility of such name-calling by saying that the circumcision of Jews was, after all, "made in the flesh by hands" (verse 11).

Circumcision was introduced in the context of God's renewed covenant with Abraham (Gen. 17). For Israelites it became a religious rite that marked them as a special people of the covenant. Moses went a step further in affirming its spiritual meaning by calling for the circumcision of the heart (Deut. 10:16). This spiritual setting apart of Israel as a special people placed them under a moral and spiritual obligation to manifest among all nations the qualities of commitment and obedience to the God of the covenant.

Circumcision was more than a physical mark; it was a mark of being consecrated to God. God's setting apart of Israel as a special people was rooted not in any special quality of Israel but in God's sovereign choice (Amos 3:2). Israel was expected to be a messenger to all nations and a channel of God's blessings to the world: "In you all the families of the earth shall be blessed" (Gen. 12:3). God "had called them [Israel] to preserve among men the knowledge of His law, and of the symbols and prophecies that pointed to the Savior. He desired them to be as wells of salvation to the world. . . . They were to reveal God to men."[1]

Unfortunately, Israel failed to fulfill that calling. What was to be a sign of allegiance to God and a constant reminder of Israel's status as the chosen vessel of blessings to all nations turned out to be a divider between Jews and Gentiles. The symbol of chosenness and the mark of spiritual and moral responsibility became a dividing wall between Jews and Gentiles.

As a result there stood an impenetrable wall between the Jew and the Gentile. Paul tells the Ephesians that Gentile Christians were subjected to the contempt of being called the "uncircumcised," but that contempt was a thing of the past. In a subtle way he reminds them not to return the favor. In Christ, the apostle wrote to the Galatians, "neither circumcision nor uncircumcision avails anything, but faith working through love" (Gal. 5:6). For what counts is not the circumcision of the flesh, but circumcision of the heart (Rom. 2:29). The former is "made in the flesh by hands" (Eph. 2:11); the latter is "made without hands, by putting off the body of the sins of the flesh, by the circumcision of Christ, buried with Him in baptism, in which you also were raised with Him through faith in the working of God, who raised Him from the dead" (Col. 2:11, 12). The former divides people; the latter unites.

Second, before coming to Christ, Gentiles were "aliens from the commonwealth of Israel and strangers from the covenants of promise" (Eph. 2:12). Without Christ life was one of spiritual alienation and poverty. Gentiles could pride themselves in all that they had—philosophy, literature, education, wealth, political positions, citizenship in the most powerful nations of the world, yet they were foreigners to the covenant promises and the messianic aspirations that God had revealed to Israel.

History is a witness to the plight of people without Christ. They could not find a way out of their spiritual predicament from all the religious systems and philosophies of the world. Only emptiness stares at those without Christ. They live life in a circle—from meaninglessness to meaninglessness. They have no answer to the problem of sin. Without Christ life is empty, bleak, and alienated.

Third, before they came to Christ, Gentiles were without hope and without God. Hope that does not spring from an abiding faith in God is not hope. The apostle was fully aware that God had revealed Himself to all humankind through many ways, including nature (Rom. 1:18, 19), but the Gentiles chose to turn to idolatry, creating "many gods" and "many lords" (1 Cor. 8:5). The city of Ephesus itself bore witness to such a self-created god, in the form of Diana. All the gods and goddesses of Rome and Greece could not fill the emptiness of the human soul or solve the problem of sin. These people believed in gods, but they had no knowledge of the true God, and so in effect they were godless. Consequently, they were without hope.

Thus ends Paul's description of life without Christ: godless, stateless, friendless, promiseless, and hopeless. Fortunately, Paul does not end there. From "at that time . . . without Christ," he turns to "now in Christ."

"Now in Christ Jesus . . ." (Ephesians 2:13-18)

"But now in Christ Jesus you who once were far off have been brought near by the blood of Christ" (Eph. 2:13). The words "far" and "near" describe the position of the Gentiles and the Jews with reference to God, and portrays life both outside of Christ and in Christ. The prophet Isaiah spoke of the Gentiles who were far off (Isa. 57:19). Moses spoke of Israel, "For what great nation is there that has God so near to it, as the Lord our God is to us?" (Deut. 4:7).

However, this nearness was not to be understood as exclusiveness, and it is here that Israel misunderstood its position with reference to Gentiles. The nearness meant that Israel had the privilege of a close and intimate connection with God; they were the recipients of God's revelation (Rom. 3:1, 2). The very nearness of Israel imposed upon them a responsibility to communicate God's will to those who were far off, and in this they failed. However, God predicted that a time would come when this difference between nearness and far off would disappear (Isa. 57:19)—a messianic prophecy pointing to the time when distance between God and all people will vanish.

To Paul, this messianic prophecy was fulfilled in Christ, who has abolished all distance by His blood (Eph. 2:13). One privilege that Jews held dear was that of being near to God's Temple, and within the Temple to the mercy seat. The sacrificial blood in the Temple rituals played a crucial role in keeping the Jews near to God's presence. The apostle moves from the blood of the animal to the blood of Christ, which bridges the gulf between God and sinners.

Paul's insight is foundational to the understanding of the gospel. To speak of blood as a means of forgiveness of sin and reconciliation with God may seem revolting to some, but the Bible offers no alternative. "Without the shedding of blood there is no forgiveness" of sin, and Christ did precisely this by "the sacrifice of himself" (Heb. 9:22, 26, NIV). Christ's shed blood on the cross is God's only way to deal with sin. Through this act "a new and living way [has] opened for us" in order that we may "draw near to God with a sincere heart in full assurance of faith" (Heb. 10:20, 22, NIV). Thus the primary integrating principle of all humanity into one is not philosophical, political, or sociological, but redemptive through the blood of Christ.

From the language of far and near, Paul moves to a more vivid picture: "For He Himself is our peace, who has made both one, and has broken down the middle wall of separation" (Eph. 2:14).

Christ's reconciling ministry on the cross made peace possible not only between God and sinners but also between hostile factions within the human family, such as Jews and Gentiles. How did Jesus accomplish this? By breaking "down the middle wall of partition" (verse 14, KJV).

What was Paul referring to by the wall of partition? The picture of the Temple in Jerusalem comes to mind. The Temple had a wall that separated the court of the Gentiles from the rest of the Temple area. In several places on that wall were signs in Greek and Roman languages warning the Gentiles to keep away. In 1871 archaeologists discovered one such sign, with this inscription: "Let no one of any other nation come within the fence and barrier around the Holy Place. Whoever will be taken doing so will himself be responsible for the fact that his death will ensue."[2]

Paul was well aware of that barrier, for he himself was arrested and sent to imprisonment in Rome on the accusation that he brought into the forbidden Temple area a Gentile, Trophimus—who, incidentally, was from Ephesus (Acts 21:28, 29).

But the "wall" in our text under study refers to more than that literal wall that cut off Gentile access to the Temple. It refers to religious, social, political, and other divisions that kept the two groups apart. We see the existence of walls everywhere in the form of race, color, caste, gender, or ideology. Wherever a person or a group is discriminated against, is excluded from friendship and fellowship, is forbidden to participate in the joy that Christ has brought about, there is a wall. That wall must be torn down. That is the cry of the cross.

So Paul writes with conviction and courage from the Roman jail. He tells the Ephesians that Christ has broken down the wall of partition that divides humanity into hostile groups. In dying for the sins of all humanity Christ brings peace in two dimensions: vertically, between God and humanity; and horizontally, between person and person, people and people. The former proclaims that God loves all alike; the later demands that in Christ "there is neither Jew nor Greek, there is neither slave nor free, there is neither male nor female; for you are all one in Christ Jesus" (Gal. 3:28).

By breaking down this wall of separation Christ has accomplished the impossible: "to create in Himself one new man from the two, thus making peace" (Eph. 2:15). Here we have the wonder of Pauline mathematics: 1 + 1 = 1. It may not make sense. It is not logical. But it is a reality grounded in the gospel, taught by Jesus, and founded on the reconciling act of Jesus on the cross.

This destruction of the wall underscores much of the ministry of Christ. His life, teachings, and finally His death established that the end result of His gospel would be the creation of a new humanity—one and undivided, reflecting the Edenic ideal of the Creator. Consider how Jesus destroyed some of those walls in His life, teachings, and death.

The story begins even before His birth. Observe His genealogy. Fond of preserving their pedigrees, the Jews set great value on purity of lineage. A priest was expected to produce a pure pedigree back to Aaron; his wife to at least five generations. To such a pedigree-conscious people, Matthew's Gospel gives the genealogy of Jesus that proclaims the Savior to be not a parochial messiah but a universal Redeemer whose mission is to restore the original design of the Creator. Matthew mentions four names in the ancestry of Jesus: Bathsheba, a Hittite; Ruth, a Moabite; Tamar and Rahab, Canaanites—all women, all Gentiles, all sinners. Bethlehem's crib affirms that in biblical anthropology there shall be no male or female, no Jew or Gentile, but only God's children.

The ministry of Jesus brought Him in touch with the entire spectrum of society. The rich young ruler, the leper down the street, Nicodemus, the Syrophoenician woman, the Pharisee, or the Greeks—it did not make any difference to the Master. In fact, throughout His ministry He broke down walls that divided people.

Not only in His relation with people but also in the establishment of

His kingdom, Jesus revealed the new order of human relations based on the worth of the individual. This comes through, among other ways, in His prescription of the new commandment, His establishment of the Lord's Supper, His cross, and His Great Commission.

The new commandment. When Jesus speaks of His new commandment of love (John 13:34), the newness refers not to love but to the object of love. People love, but they love the lovable; they love their own. Jesus introduced a new factor: "Just as I have loved you, you should also love one another." That is to say, just as universal, as sacrificial, and as complete as Jesus' love is, so should our love be. On that type of love "hang all the law and the prophets" (Matt. 22:40, KJV).

The command to love our neighbor leaves absolutely no room for modification. We do not select those whom we love; we are called upon to love all. As children of one Father we are expected to love one another. In the parable of the good Samaritan Christ has shown that "our neighbor does not mean merely one of the church or faith to which we belong. It has no reference to race, color, or class distinction. Our neighbor is every person who needs our help. Our neighbor is every soul who is wounded and bruised by the adversary. Our neighbor is everyone who is the property of God."[3]

The ordinance of the Lord's Supper. "Because there is one bread," Paul wrote to the Corinthians, "we who are many are one body, for we all partake of the one bread" (1 Cor. 10:17, RSV). The bread and the wine are symbols of the broken body and spilt blood of Jesus, which brought about reconciliation, both vertical and horizontal. To sit at that table and at the same time discriminate against another human being is a desecration of God's family.

The cross. As God's instrument of redemption and reconciliation the cross brings back what was lost in Eden—the restoration of the image of God with, among other things, the reality of human togetherness and unity. At the foot of the cross the ground is level. Through the cross God "was reconciling the world to himself" (2 Cor. 5:19, RSV). "The Cross is God's best picture of himself. . . . It is the place where God comes to grips with the forces that violate his love; it becomes the place where he draws men into harmony with the love and the purposes that flow from it. . . . The reconciliation of man to man, through the reconciliation of man to God, releases the healing power of God into this anxious, broken, and bitter world. Only redeemed men can reconcile."[4]

The Great Commission. Both the Great Commission (Matt. 28:19,

20; Mark 16:15, 16; Acts 1:8) and the message of Revelation 14:6-12 envision the creation of a world family. Evangelism is Christ's antidote for prejudice within the church. Where there is a strong evangelistic program, where there is a burden for winning souls, there will be a universal feeling for men and women of every kind. True evangelists see the world as their parish; they do not recognize frontiers and restrictions that divide communities. Paul must become an apostle to the Gentiles, Peter must go to Cornelius, Barnabas must go to Antioch, Philip must rush to Samaria, Philemon must take back Onesimus. The blood of Christ is the ink with which the covenant of brotherhood is written.

When we take Jesus to the world, we cannot afford to build a church with walls. Indeed, the proclamation of the good news of Jesus and having a church with a dividing wall are mutually contradictory. For Christ has "abolished in His flesh" (Eph. 2:15) (that is, on the cross) every law that was against the unity of humanity. The law does not refer to the Ten Commandments, for that is the moral code that governs humanity. Nothing in that law is against the Gentile. The law that was abolished on the cross refers to the ceremonial law, including circumcision, on the basis of which the Jewish world erected a middle wall of partition and kept the Gentiles away.

Thus the twin act of the cross—Christ's dying for our sin and reconciling us to God and one another, and the abolishment of all ceremonies that were part of the middle wall—ensures peace to both Jews and Gentiles. And both have direct "access by one Spirit to the Father" (verse 18).

"Now, Therefore . . ." (Ephesians 2:19-22)

The final step in Paul's argument of this new creation of one united body out of two hostile bodies is a description of the present status of Gentiles. Because they have accepted Christ they receive certain privileges that were not theirs at one time. Three such privileges are mentioned.

First, citizenship. No longer "strangers and foreigners," the Gentiles in Christ have become "fellow citizens" (verse 19). At one time Gentiles were rootless wanderers, spiritually speaking; they had no stability or status. But now, in Christ, they have a "new birth" certificate. They are born into the kingdom of God. And hence, they are citizens. Citizenship makes them equal with other saints. Both Jews and Gentiles, Greeks and barbarians, educated and illiterate, male and female, possess the same citizenship, and both belong to the same kingdom (see Phil. 3:20, 21).

Second, a family. Coming to Christ makes us "members of the household of God" (Eph. 2:19). This metaphor is more personal and intimate. A kingdom is one thing; a family is another. From the wider circle of the kingdom, Christ brings us to a more intimate closeness of family. To be a citizen is a precious privilege, but to be a child is not only a privilege but also an experience of love and affection from the Father. In Christ, life undergoes a new creation—the prodigal becomes a child, the stranger becomes a citizen, the starved and the dying sit at the table of the Father and receive the enduring gift of acceptance and life.

Third, a temple. The imagery of the temple is awesome: it has been built on the foundations of the prophets and the apostles, and its chief cornerstone is Christ Himself (verse 20). Into that spiritually challenging architecture we are "being built together for a dwelling place of God in the Spirit" (verse 22).

Translate all this imagery, and what do we have? Two concepts, both of which place a supreme responsibility on the life of the Christian. On a personal level each Christian is a temple of God, a dwelling place for the Spirit. "Do you not know," says the apostle, "that you are the temple of God and that the Spirit of God dwells in you? If anyone defiles the temple of God, God will destroy him. For the temple of God is holy, which temple you are" (1 Cor. 3:16, 17). Here is the essential challenge of life in Christ. As the living abode of God's Spirit, must we not keep ourselves—our mind, our spirit, our body—pure and sanctified? Life in Christ is a call to a life of holiness.

On a corporate level Christians do not live independent of one another. We belong to the body of Christ, the community of faith. That's what we call the church, and it is in that corporate level that we are challenged to live the life of the cross—that great means through which God has destroyed the middle wall of partition. A "dwelling place of God in the Spirit" cannot be a center of division and hostility.

---

[1] E. G. White, *The Desire of Ages,* p. 27.

[2] In W. Barclay, *The Letters to the Galatians and the Ephesians,* p. 112.

[3] White, *The Desire of Ages,* p. 503.

[4] *The Interpreter's Bible* (Nashville: Abingdon Press, 1980), vol. 10, pp. 525, 526.

CHAPTER 7

The Mystery of God

Ephesians 3

The third chapter of Ephesians begins with Paul's self-description: "the prisoner of Christ Jesus." Two points of interest need to be noted. Paul could have introduced himself as a "prisoner of Nero," for that's what he was. But the apostle transcends the plight of the present to grasp higher, more nobler truths. A true Christian does that; earth does not bind him or her; he or she always looks up to heaven. So Paul identifies himself as a "prisoner of Christ Jesus" (Eph. 3:1).

The second interesting point is that Paul calls himself "the prisoner . . . for you Gentiles" (verse 1). Literally, that's true, for one of the charges against him is that he brought into the Temple in Jerusalem an Ephesian Gentile. Paul attributes his imprisonment with these words: "For this reason" (verse 1). The reason can be traced back to Ephesians 2, where he proclaims that in Jesus there is neither Jew nor Gentile. That call for unity is often a cause for offense—it was so in Paul's time, and it is so in our own. But it takes courage to stand for a Christian principle, and the apostle risked his life for the principle of the broken wall.

The prisoner in Rome now presents the gospel of new creation and transformed relationships under the label "mystery." Chapter 3 speaks of the contents of the mystery, the purpose of the mystery, and the gratitude to this mystery.

The Contents of the Mystery (Ephesians 3:1-7)

As noted earlier, the New Testament does not use the word "mystery" as something hidden or secretive. Mystery, to Paul, is something we have not known in the past but God has revealed to us. Both the content and the purpose of this mystery are incomprehensible to the human mind without divine revelation and assistance. Paul identifies the divine mystery with the revelation of God in Christ (Col. 2:2; Eph. 1:9).

Another characteristic of this mystery is that generations that had lived before the coming of Christ were not fully aware of it (Eph. 3:5). God chose to reveal it fully in the person of Christ, and Paul was a recipient of this revelation. Ephesians adds clarity to the understanding of this mystery in four ways.

First, the revelation of this mystery in Christ is God's sovereign act. God has "made known to us the mystery of His will, according to His good pleasure which He purposed in Himself" (Eph. 1:9). No human being could have thought of the redemptive plan, much less executed it, but God has revealed this plan through Christ so that through Him "He might gather together in one all things in Christ" (verse 10).

Second, the apostle links this mystery of unity to God's grace (Eph. 3:2). Once again, human helplessness stands out. Scholars before and after Paul have written about unity, but usually it is unity within a single group, often against another group. No Greek philosopher, no Roman poet, no Jewish rabbi, no Hindu pandit, no Buddhist monk, has written about unity of differing people groups—free and slave, Greeks and barbarians, Jew and Gentile, Brahman and the untouchable. But the biblical concept of unity, the one that Paul calls the mystery of God, is a result of divine revelation through Jesus Christ on the cross. It took the divine act of the cross to break down the walls of partition, providing forgiveness and reconciliation to all humankind in the same manner.

A wartime story is told of some French soldiers who took the body of a fallen comrade for burial. It was late in the evening when they knocked on the door of the priest in whose parish was the cemetery. The priest was willing to bury the body, but first he had a question. "Was he a Roman Catholic?" Only Roman Catholics could be buried in that cemetery.

"We don't know," said the soldiers.

"I'm sorry," said the priest, "but I cannot bury him in our cemetery." Disappointed, the soldiers dug a grave outside the cemetery, buried their comrade, and went back to their barracks. Next morning they returned to see if everything was all right, but they could not locate the grave of their comrade. They searched and searched, to no avail.

Just then the priest came out of the church and told the soldiers, "All night I was burdened and grieving over my refusal. The rules say that no one who is not a Catholic may be buried in the cemetery, but the rules do not say that I can't move the fence. So I moved the fence to include the grave of a brave soldier." Where the spirit of Christ reigns, fences must be moved to provide inclusion.

Third, Paul says that this mystery was revealed to him. The apostle never claimed that he discovered the truth of salvation by grace. Nor did he ever say that he discovered the truth of the broken wall. This truth, the horizontal and vertical aspects of reconciliation, came to him as a revelation on the road to Damascus (Acts 9:1-15). From then on he never doubted his call to be an apostle to Gentiles, to invite the Gentiles to be part of the universal fellowship that Christ has established.

Fourth, Paul's grasp of this mystery was so total and complete that he devoted his life entirely to its proclamation. So far as the apostle was concerned, the inclusion of the Gentiles in God's new creation was complete and unconditional. God's redemptive grace had made it possible that the "Gentiles should be fellow heirs, of the same body, and partakers of His promise in Christ through the gospel" (Eph. 3:6). Those who at one time were aliens and strangers, without hope and without God, now, thanks to God's grace, have become fellow heirs, members of the same body, and sharers of the same hope. The gospel of Jesus makes no difference between various people groups; it recognizes only one new creation of a new humanity.

Outside the gospel there is no answer to the question of splintered humanity. History has recorded many human attempts to bring about unity. Greeks talked in terms of "eternal recurrence" and the universal mind; Romans turned to law, language, and civilization; Marx projected classless economics; Nietzsche built his superman; Hindus have their cyclic karma—but none of these or any other attempt could do away with sin, the root cause for disharmony between God and human, and between people and people. Biblical revelation alone has the solution that shatters the wall and creates a fellowship in which all humanity can sit at the table of brotherhood. That solution is the gospel of Jesus Christ. Of this gospel—this mystery—Paul considered himself to be a servant, a steward, a minister (verse 7).

The Purpose of the Mystery (Ephesians 3:8-13)

In saying that God had revealed this mystery to him, Paul was not being proud or self-assertive. In fact, there is an element of wonder on the part of the apostle as to why God should have called him at all to this ministry, he being "less than the least of all the saints" (Eph. 3:8). Why would God choose a legalist to proclaim free grace, a "gestapo" agent against the early church to be Christianity's greatest defender, a Pharisee of the Pharisees to be an apostle to the Gentiles? The call to ministry is always a wonder. The effectiveness of that ministry depends on never forgetting the source and the purpose of the calling.

What was the purpose of this mystery? Paul outlines a threefold purpose.

The first purpose is the creation of a new humanity (Eph. 2:15). The gathering in of the Jews and the Gentiles created a new fellowship called the church, the body of Christ (Eph. 1:23). Through Christ all may become part of that body. The church itself is a fellowship of believers who have heard and accepted the "unsearchable riches of Christ" (Eph. 3:8).

The riches of Christ are unsearchable, but not in the sense of being hidden or being beyond understanding. Rather, they are unsearchable because they are abundant, beyond human estimate, and can never be exhausted. His love, grace, mercy, forgiveness, enabling, justification, sanctification—the list can go on—are beyond what human imagination can think, plan, or aspire. Indeed, Christ not only possesses unsearchable riches and empowers us with these, but He Himself is our riches, and in Him we find a sufficiency beyond what we can imagine.

Perhaps the most important element of the unsearchableness of His riches is His death on our behalf that we may be saved, and having been saved we may be united with one another and with God.

The second purpose of the mystery revealed through Christ is the cosmic vindication of the name and character of God. The church as a community of faith with no dividing wall in its midst is heaven's showpiece of what the gospel can do to a divided humanity. It is a cosmic exhibit of His power (Eph. 1:19), His grace (Eph. 2:7), and His "wisdom," which defeated the divisive forces of Satan, "according to the eternal purpose which He accomplished in Christ Jesus our Lord" (Eph. 3:10, 11). It is through the church—the new creation of God—that the "principalities and powers in the heavenly places" come to know what the "manifold wisdom of God" has "accomplished in Christ Jesus" (verses 10, 11).

"Our Lord designed that His church should reflect to the world the fullness and sufficiency that we find in Him. We are constantly receiving of God's bounty, and by imparting of the same we are to represent to the world the love and beneficence of Christ. . . . We are members of His mystical body. He is the head, controlling all the members of the body. Jesus Himself, in His infinite mercy, is working on human hearts, effecting spiritual transformations so amazing that angels look on with astonishment and joy."[1]

The apostle says that all "principalities and powers," meaning all created intelligences, fallen and unfallen, are interested in the outcome of

God's plan of reconciliation. In agreement with Paul is Peter. Describing what God's love, wisdom, and grace have accomplished—the defeat of Satan and the salvation of the human race—Peter notes that these were "things which angels desire to look into" (1 Peter 1:12). "Our little world is the lesson book of the universe. God's wonderful purpose of grace, the mystery of redeeming love, is the theme into which 'angels desire to look,' and it will be their study throughout endless ages."[2]

But why should this be of interest to Satan and his cohorts? The answer must be found in the theme of the great controversy that is so central to an understanding of the biblical portrayal of a loving God in search of His lost children. When Lucifer rebelled against God and was cast out of heaven, along with his followers (Rev. 12:7-9), the preeminent issue was the character of God as manifest in His law, love, and justice.

Satan's charge both in heaven and on earth has been that God's law is arbitrary and cannot be kept, and that His love is contradictory to justice. With a third of heaven's angels on his side and with the disobedience of Adam and Eve—and through them the human race—Satan seemed to have triumphed. Ever since that tragedy in Eden, Satan's primary work has been to keep the human race in bondage to sin, perpetuating the charge that God's law cannot be kept, and that God cannot be loving and just at the same time. Justice demands death—how can God be just and yet forgive the sinner?

Satan's cosmic challenge had its fitting answer in the plan of redemption that God conceived before the foundation of the world (Eph. 1:4; 3:9). "Through Christ's redeeming work the government of God stands justified. The Omnipotent One is made known as the God of love. Satan's charges are refuted, and his character unveiled. Rebellion can never again arise. Sin can never again enter the universe. Through eternal ages all are secure from apostasy. By love's self-sacrifice, the inhabitants of earth and heaven are bound to their Creator in bonds of indissoluble union."[3]

This "indissoluble union" stands as a rebuke to Satan and his angels. Satan experienced the sting of death on the cross, and he shudders at what the body of Christ, united and victorious, can do to his diabolic plans to misguide human beings. Indeed, the "unsearchable riches of Christ" manifested through the church stand as an indictment of the evil forces in the universe.

As participants in this cosmic exhibit of God's workings, we have both a privilege and a responsibility. Our privilege is to be faithful to the fellowship of the new creation; our responsibility is to "resist" the devil (1 Peter 5:9), and let God's eternal purpose of reconciliation be realized in our relationships and in our conduct.

Third, the purpose of the mystery of the gospel is to throw open the doors and let us have direct access to God (Eph. 3:12). Before their fall, Adam and Eve had direct, free communion with God. By their sin they lost open access to God. But now through the plan of redemption, humanity has entered into a new status, an intimate relationship, marked by bold and confident and direct access to God without any intermediary, be it a priest or a saint or a rite. The cross makes possible God's approachability. "Let us therefore come boldly to the throne of grace, that we may obtain mercy and find grace to help in time of need" (Heb. 4:16).

Gratitude for the Mystery (Ephesians 3:13-21)

Paul now comes to the final section of his study on the mystery of God—a prayer of gratitude to God for this great revelation. The prayer acknowledges the greatness and goodness of God. That should be the immediate response of all the redeemed. "For this reason," says Paul (Eph. 3:14)—that is, for the reason of the gospel that brought about forgiveness, reconciliation, and unity. It's reason enough to drive one to one's knees. That was Paul's position. In humble submission and gratitude, the apostle offers a prayer of thanksgiving and appreciation to the Father and the Son, who made the creation of the new family possible.

What is this family? It has a name, the name of Jesus Christ (verses 14, 15). It's an inclusive name. All in heaven and all the redeemed on this earth together constitute this family that carries the precious name of the Savior. The Christian family is thus a universal family that acknowledges Jesus Christ as its Lord and Savior. A day is coming—and surely it will come soon—when the entire universe, all the created intelligences, including the fallen angels and unrepentant sinners, will acknowledge the supremacy of that name. That was Paul's conclusion in Philippians: "Therefore God also has highly exalted Him and given Him the name which is above every name, that at the name of Jesus every knee should bow, of those in heaven, and of those on earth, and of those under the earth, and that every tongue should confess that Jesus Christ is Lord, to the glory of God the Father" (Phil. 2:9-11).

That universal acknowledgment of the Lordship of Christ, which concludes the great controversy between Christ and Satan, is the final objective of the mystery of the gospel. The apostle is grateful for what God has accomplished for our salvation, and he expresses that gratitude in prayer (Eph. 3:14-21).

First, he prays for the strengthening of the inner being (verse 16). The strength of the community of God's people, as seen in its unity of life and witness, is an important part of this gospel of new relationships. Just as important is the strength of the inner life of each believer. For the Greeks the "inner man" referred to reason, conscience, and will. To Paul, the inner being is the center of one's personality, where critical decisions are made and where the soul's decisive battles are won or lost. Paul knows that whoever occupies that inner seat controls the individual. Hence Paul prays that Christ may "dwell in your hearts through faith" (verse 17). The Greek word for "dwell" is *katoikeo,* indicating "to reside permanently." We need Christ not as a guest but as a permanent part of our lives. He becomes the controlling power of our lives—to guide, direct, counsel, and comfort.

Second, the apostle prays for full comprehension of the mystery in all its dimensions—the width, length, depth, and height of Christ's love (verse 18). Such comprehension is not a one-person journey in the land of solitude; it is accomplished "with all the saints" (verse 18). Individual prayer, study, and meditation are important and must not be minimized. But a person whose primary interest is God will not choose to live the life of a lonely meditator. Rather, such a person will affirm oneness with other saints—celebrating God's love with them, sharing insights from God's Word with each other, praying and worshipping together. That is one sure way of comprehending and living the "fullness of God" (verse 19).

That comprehension is more than a lifelong task; it will be the study of eternity. My wife and I have been married for 44 years. We have walked hand in hand, marched through life's joys and concerns, defeats and victories, struggles and triumphs. Yet neither of us can say we know all there is to know about each other. Neither can claim to know what the other thinks. Neither can predict the ups and downs of love's intimate journey. How much more to know and appreciate the love of God!

"The theme of redemption . . . will be the science and the song of the redeemed throughout the ceaseless ages of eternity. Is it not worthy of careful thought and study now? . . . As we thus contemplate heavenly themes, our faith and love will grow stronger, and our prayers will be more and more acceptable to God, because they will be more and more mixed with faith and love. They will be intelligent and fervent. There will be more constant confidence in Jesus, and a daily, living experience in His power to save to the uttermost all that come unto God by Him."[4]

Such dynamic possibilities exist for the Christian community, not only in the future home to come but even now. Our God is one "who is able to do exceedingly abundantly above all that we ask or think" (verse 20). His love is limitless. His grace is unfathomable. His promises are exceedingly precious and abundant. He is the God who makes the impossible possible. Has He not created one new creation out of two humanities? To Him, therefore, "be glory in the church by Christ Jesus to all generations, forever and ever. Amen" (verse 21).

---

[1] Ellen G. White, *Testimonies for the Church* (Mountain View, Calif.: Pacific Press Pub. Assn., 1948), vol. 5, p. 731.

[2] White, *The Desire of Ages,* p. 19.

[3] *Ibid.,* p. 26.

[4] Ellen G. White, *Steps to Christ* (Nashville: Southern Pub. Assn., 1949), pp. 88, 89.

CHAPTER 8

The Worthy Walk

Ephesians 4:1-16

I point you," says Ellen White, "to the words of the apostle Paul in the fourth chapter of Ephesians. This whole chapter is a lesson that God desires us to learn and practice."[1]

In chapters 1 to 3 of Ephesians Paul narrated the story of God's plan of salvation. Can one be saved by believing in a doctrine? The answer is obvious. John Wesley once said that "the devils believe, and still remain devils." Correctness of knowledge or the volume of our knowledge or the ability to defend the truthfulness of our knowledge about Jesus will not bring about new creation. Reconciliation and new creation are a result of accepting Jesus as our Lord and Savior: coming to Him, placing our lives in His trust, walking as He walked, living as He lived, abiding in Him without any deviation or hesitation—all by His grace and power.

Doctrine is important, but it must move beyond the intellectual level to the practical. Paul does just that, beginning with chapter 4. He proceeds from theology to practice, from exposition to exhortation, from what God has done to what we should do. Hence Paul turns his attention to the lifestyle of believers, to a "walk worthy of the calling" (verse 1). The rest of the Epistle deals with the Christian walk.

How Paul begins his appeal to Christians about living out their faith is noteworthy: "I, therefore, the prisoner of the Lord, beseech you to walk worthly of the calling with which you were called" (verse 1). The word "therefore" refers to the doctrine of redemption, reconciliation, and unity outlined in chapters 1 to 3. Doctrine is not an empty rhetoric; it is the "therefore," the foundation, the basis of Christian ethics and practice. What God has done demands a lifestyle response from us. The appeal, in the form of an earnest "beseeching," comes from the "prisoner of the Lord" who introduced himself in the same way as he presented the great truth of the mystery (Eph. 3:1). Arising from the new life that flows from that mystery is the demand for the worthy walk, and it is presented in Ephesians 4:1-16 in terms of its characteristics, its purpose, and its empowerment.

The Worthy Walk: Its Characteristics (Ephesians 4:1, 2)

The Greek word for "worthy" is *axios*. Its root meaning refers to a balance, as on scales. The Christian practice must stand in balance with Christian belief and profession. Nothing hurts Christian life and witness as much as a lack of balance, a lack of consistency. Mahatma Gandhi once said, "Show me a Christian and I will become one." That is the challenge of evangelism and proclamation. It is easier for one to believe that the gospel is the power of God to transform lives when one sees that power in changed lives. An exemplary life speaks louder than a thousand words.

Augustine, who once lived a life of sin and debauchery, found his Savior and dedicated his life to Christian service and ministry. One day he was walking down the street when one of his former mistresses called out to him, "Augustine, come here." But Augustine did not turn back. Again, the same seductive voice. Still Augustine kept walking. Finally, the woman shouted, "Augustine, it is I."

Without turning around, the great Christian shouted back, "But it is not I," and went on his way. A worthy walk is a transformed, consistent walk. "The worldling and the infidel admire consistency and have ever been powerfully convicted that God was of a truth with His people when their works correspond with their faith. 'By their fruits ye shall know them.' Every tree is known by its own fruits. Our words, our actions, are the fruit we bear."[2]

Paul's emphasis is that we "walk worthy of the calling." The apostle mentions five foundational graces that must mark the Christian life and walk.

The first grace is lowliness (Eph. 4:2). The New International Version translates: "Be completely humble." The culture of Paul's day—both Roman and Greek—considered humility a sign of weakness. Greek literature makes no reference to humility as a virtue; rather, it associates humility with slavishness, subservience, lack of will, ignobility, cringing, and low self-esteem. Against such cultural impediments Paul calls upon the Christian to be humble and gentle.

Paul's call is in line with biblical teachings. Isaiah describes God as both transcendent and immanent. He is "the High and Lofty One who inhabits eternity, whose name is Holy: . . . [the One who dwells] with him who has a contrite and humble spirit" (Isa. 57:15). It is the mind of humility that motivated Jesus to empty Himself and take the form of a servant—*doulos,* a bond servant—and humble Himself to the point of death in order to reveal the mystery of salvation (Phil. 2:2-8). Humility is a sign of true religion (Micah 6:8), and it is necessary to enter the kingdom of God (Matt. 5:3).

In contrast, the Bible also notes that it was pride and self-assertion that led to the fall of Lucifer, whose continuous chorus was "I will, I will, I will," in opposition to God's will (see Isa. 14:12-15). Pride goes before destruction (Prov. 16:18); it does not seek God (Ps. 10:4). Hence God is opposed to the proud (Prov. 3:34; James 4:6).

The second grace is meekness. Meekness and humility are inseparable, but meekness carries a sense of being gentle, sensitive, thoughtful, and tolerant of the other person. Far from indicative of a weak disposition, meekness marks a quiet, inner strength. Moses was said to be the meekest of all men (Num. 12:3), but he was no spineless leader.

The Greek word for meekness is *praus,* which was often used to denote an animal that was completely trained and fully under control. Therefore it might be said that a person who is *praus* is well trained and under control. A God-controlled person will certainly be meek, "in honour preferring one another" (Rom. 12:10, KJV).

Then there is the grace of "long-suffering," or patience. The Bible repeatedly uses patience and long-suffering as characteristics of God in His dealings with humanity. Peter refers to God's patience with a world in rebellion during the time of Noah (1 Peter 3:20). He also says "that the longsuffering of our Lord is salvation" (2 Peter 3:15). If God had been like us, He would have long ago wiped out humanity from the universe, but instead He waits patiently for us. The apostle even suggests that the second coming of Christ is delayed, not because God is slack in His promises, but because He "is longsuffering toward us, not willing that any should perish but that all should come to repentance" (verse 9).

The Christian must endure in the face of affliction, be tolerant in times of injustice, and be slow to anger, refusing to avenge wrongs. Patience is a characteristic of the last generation of Christians (Rev. 14:12).

Next, we come to the grace of "bearing with one another" (Eph. 4:2). This does not mean "putting up with one another," nor does it mean mutual tolerance. It involves understanding the other person and a willingness to forgive and accept one another. It is patience in action. It bears the burden another imposes, and does not yield to the temptation of taking revenge, even when such revenge is within reach.

The final grace of the worthy walk of a Christian is love, the crown jewel of the Christian life. Without it other characteristics have neither the power nor the motivation to function. It is love—agape, self-sacrificing love—that gives birth to and sustains all other graces of Christian life: humility, gentleness, patience, bearing with one another. "This *agape* is a thing, not only of the emotions, but also of the will. It is the ability to retain good will to the unlovely and the unlovable, towards those who do not love us, and even towards those whom we do not like. *Agape* is that quality of mind and heart which compels a Christian never to feel any bitterness, never feel any desire for revenge, but always to seek the highest good of every man no matter what he may be."[3]

The Worthy Walk: Its Purpose (Ephesians 4:3-6)

While the characteristics of the worthy walk are humility, gentleness, patience, forbearance, and love, the purpose of that walk is "endeavoring to keep the unity of the Spirit in the bond of peace" (Eph. 4:3). The unity and peace that Paul expects of all Christians call for right relationships. After all, Ephesians is a gospel of right relationships between humans and God, and between people and people.

How will this unity and peace be maintained? Look at the five foundational graces of the Christian life again. All have one common ingredient—each demands the death of self. So long as self is at the center the other is somewhere outside, and oneness cannot occur. If self is predominant in the church—self-glory, self-seeking, self-satisfaction—the church is only a society of fragmented beings. Its claim of oneness in the Lord is nothing but a sham and a hypocrisy. When self dies, the other person comes into focus, and the Lordship and sovereignty of Christ become supreme in the community of faith. Only then can we have "peace . . . , which passeth all understanding" (Phil. 4:7, KJV) and unity that is the envy of the world and the mystery into which all cosmic intelligences love to look into.

In the first century the Romans, both the persecutors and the silent admirers, said of the Christians, "How they love each other, and how much they are united." Unity is an inevitable fruit of love.

Paul repeats the formula of "one" seven times: "one body and one Spirit, just as you were called in one hope of your calling; one Lord, one faith, one baptism; one God and Father of all, who is above all, and through all, and in you all" (Eph. 4:4-6). Everything about Christian faith and life is one. *One God* through *one Lord* has redeemed us from sin, given to us *one faith,* regenerated us through *one Spirit,* made us members of *one body* through *one baptism,* and has given to us *one eternal hope.*

In our study of this sevenfold formula for oneness, another significant factor begs our attention. Redemption and unity are so high in God's priority that the entire Godhead is involved in creating the oneness of the church, His body. This is in keeping with the spirit of the Epistle, which so often emphasizes the entire Trinity at work in effecting the ministry of reconciliation. So we are not alone when we work for reconciliation and unity in the body of Christ. The entire Godhead is backing our work. Observe from the table below the functional aspect of each oneness:

Christian Oneness

Ingredients	**What Each Means**
one body	fellowship with the redeemed community
one Spirit	the Holy Spirit, our regenerating, sanctifying agency
one hope	the hope of eternal life, to which we are called
one Lord	Jesus, in whom alone we have redemption from sin
one faith	that which defines who we are, what we believe
one baptism	the public witness that we belong to God's family
one God and Father	our Father, in whom all things consist

Paul begins his lesson on unity with what God's reconciling mission has created through Christ—His body, the church. God created only one body of believers. There are no national, geographic, racial, ethnic, doctrinal, or linguistic bodies. Christ is the head—the operative power and intelligence of the body. He is the center of our thinking, the motive for our behavior, the controlling authority of our functions.

Second, Paul speaks of one Spirit. The Holy Spirit shows us the truth, convicts us of sin, and dwells within us (John 16:8-14; 14:15-18). His is the power by which we are regenerated. It is also by that one Spirit that we are "all baptized into one body—whether Jews or Greeks, whether slaves or free—and have all been made to drink into one Spirit" (1 Cor. 12:13). Unless individual Christians seek to live constantly under the direction of this one Spirit, Christian unity will be elusive.

Dwight L. Moody once said that to divide is the spirit of the evil one;

to unite is the ministry of the Holy Spirit. Whenever the ugly head of disunity pops up, it will be good for us to ask whose spirit is behind such forces.

Third, there is one hope. As Paul noted already (Eph. 2:12), outside of Christ we have no hope. Christ and what He has accomplished on the cross is the basis of our hope of salvation now and our hope for the future, when Christ will give us an inheritance in"heavenly places." Both redemption from sin and a place in God's eternal home are rooted in Christ (1 Peter 1:21; Titus 1:2). The second coming of Christ, therefore, is called the "blessed hope" of every Christian.

Then, there is one Lord. When Paul wrote this Epistle to the Ephesians, Caesar worship was already in existence. Before long, Christians were to choose between Christ and Caesar as their lord. To believe in Jesus and to claim Him as Lord and Savior was to make a choice between life and death. It was not an easy choice to make; in fact, one made that choice knowing that the result could well be persecution or death. But the Christian has no option but to confess the oneness and the exclusiveness of Jesus. There may be many gods and many lords, as Paul says, but to us "there is but one Lord, Jesus Christ, through whom all things came and through whom we live" (1 Cor. 8:6, NIV).

In an age that worships a multiplicity of gods not only of various religions but of other competing forces—materialism, humanism, agnosticism, intellectualism, science, New Age, technology, etc.—the Christian is called upon to confess Christ as the one Lord. And this confession admits no compromise, no competition. "There is salvation in no one else, for there is no other name under heaven given among men by which we must be saved" (Acts 4:12, RSV).

Confession of Jesus as Lord and Savior naturally results in one faith. By "faith" Paul refers not only to the act of faith in Christ that leads to salvation but also to "the faith which was once for all delivered to the saints" (Jude 3). Both the object and the subject of that faith is Jesus. He is faith's content and core, and it is therefore essential that all our faith and belief center in Him and derive authority from His Word. Traditions, worldly influences, human conveniences, so-called intellectual questioning, and similar factors that minimize the Lordship of Christ as Creator and Redeemer can have no place in the confession or proclamation of one faith. We are called to one faith and one truth—that is, as in Jesus (Eph. 4:21).

Then, there is one baptism. During his early ministry at Ephesus Paul raised the question of baptism with the few believers who were there. They had experienced the baptism of John; now Paul directed their attention to what the Baptist himself preached: "They should believe on Him who would come after him, that is, on Christ Jesus" (Acts 19:4). After that, they were baptized in the name of Jesus and received the Holy Spirit.

So the Ephesians were now aware of at least two kinds of baptisms, that of John and that of Jesus. The apostle writes to the church that in reality there is one baptism only—which is to say, the baptism of Jesus has superseded the baptism of John. John called sinners to repent and be baptized, but Jesus, along with calling for repentance, also calls upon us to believe in Him as Savior and then be baptized. Hence the commission of Jesus: "Go therefore and make disciples of all the nations, baptizing them in the name of the Father and of the Son and of the Holy Spirit" (Matt. 28:19).

Just as the apostle emphasized "one baptism," referring to the baptism of Jesus, so we too must be careful in upholding the oneness of this important rite of the church. In our context the oneness includes both the mode of baptism—by immersion (the New Testament says nothing about any other kind)—and the prelude to baptism, which is the acceptance of Jesus as Savior and of His teachings (hence a child who cannot exercise faith cannot be baptized).

Finally, the apostle speaks of "one God and Father of all, who is above all, and through all, and in you all" (Eph. 4:6). To Paul the primacy and the oneness of God are a truth out of which everything flows. Standing on an Athenian hill, he gave a basic doctrine of God: He is the Creator. "He is Lord of heaven and earth. . . . He gives to all life, breath, and all things. And He has made from one blood every nation of men to dwell on all the face of the earth, and has determined their preappointed times and the boundaries of their dwellings, so that they should seek the Lord, in the hope that they might grope for Him and find Him, though He is not far from each one of us; for in Him we live and move and have our being" (Acts 17:24-28).

If we deny God's creatorship, if we reject His Lordship and sovereignty, if we doubt His saving and sustaining role in the affairs of the human race, if we refuse to seek Him, if we deny the unity and equality of His children, what have we? Nothing.

The Worthy Walk: Its Empowerment (Ephesians 4:7-11)

Thus far in the fourth chapter Paul has given us an outline of the characteristics of the worthy walk to which Christians are called (verses 1-3). The apostle also reminded us of the characteristics of the unity that marks the Christian life in the sevenfold formula of oneness (verses 4-6). Now in verses

7 to 16 the apostle deals with God's empowerment of the Christian to do this Christian walk. The Lord who commands His followers to walk worthy is the same one who has given varied spiritual gifts to enable the Christians, both as individuals and as a corporate body, to live responsibly and for God's glory. From unity Paul moves to the uniqueness of their blessings.

But first we need to note several factors about these gifts. For one thing, they are gifts of grace given by Christ (verse 7). Christ is the giver; we are the receivers. Grace is the motivation; service is the purpose. Since Christ gives these spiritual gifts as an act of His sovereign grace to believers, it is not for the recipients to question the gift. Gifts are given according to God's discernment. We can neither demand nor prescribe conditions for their receipt.

Another point to note is this difficult passage: "Therefore He says: 'When He ascended on high, He led captivity captive, and gave gifts to men.' (Now this, 'He ascended'—what does it mean but that He also first descended into the lower parts of the earth? He who descended is also the One who ascended far above all the heavens, that He might fill all things)" (verses 8-10).

The first part—"when He ascended on high" He gave gifts to men—is clear. Before His ascension Jesus told the disciples to wait in Jerusalem until they received the Spirit and were equipped to witness for the gospel (Acts 1:4). They did tarry, the Spirit did come, and the Pentecost and proclamation are a matter of history. The Holy Spirit and the accompanying gifts to the church were the coronation gift of the risen Jesus, given when He "ascended on high" (Eph. 4:8).

But what is one to make of these words: "He also first descended into the lower parts of the earth. He who descended is also the One who ascended far above all the heavens" (verses 9, 10)? The contrast between "descended" and "ascended" is not spatial but theological. "Lower parts of the earth" refers not to any spatial location inside or beneath the earth, but to the depths of humiliation that Jesus underwent in His incarnation and crucifixion experience on this earth.

For Christ, who was God, coming to the earth, walking in our midst, and suffering Gethsemane and the cross—these were the depths of humiliation. Paul uses the metaphor the "lower parts of the earth" to describe that humbling of Christ for the sake of us sinners. The metaphor may also be understood as Jesus taking the battle of the great controversy to the very headquarters of the devil. It is theologically the darkest of darkness and metaphorically the lower parts of the earth—and gaining a crushing victory over the old serpent.

Christ's descent was thus complete, but, thanks to the power of resurrection, His ascent was even greater. By His victory over Satan He "ascended far above all the heavens" and fills all things. Because He descended to the point of death, having left the exalted position held in heaven as equal to God, He was coronated upon His ascension as the Lord and sovereign of the universe, at whose feet all will bow (Phil. 2:10). From this exalted position Christ is linked with the church on earth so closely that He fills her with gifts.

The gifts vary from one recipient to another. "He Himself gave some to be apostles, some prophets, some evangelists, and some pastors and teachers" (Eph. 4:11). The variety of gifts does not indicate the superiority or inferiority of the believers. "To each one of us grace was given according to the measure of Christ's gift" (verse 7). No one who belongs to Christ is left without a spiritual gift. All are called, all are gifted, and all are to serve. "[Eph. 4:11] shows that there are to be different workers, different instrumentalities. Each has a different work. No one is required to lay hold of another's work, and, though untrained, try to do it. God has given to each according to his ability."[4]

Four gifts are mentioned in Ephesians. **Paul first lists apostles;** these are the ones whom Jesus called to be eyewitnesses of His ministry, the ones who received the charge to proclaim the gospel and establish the church. Originally the term indicated the 12 disciples; later Paul was specifically called to be an apostle to the Gentiles (Acts 9:15, 16). He always made plain that the calling was neither his invention nor anyone else's bestowal, but that of the risen Jesus (Rom. 1:1; 1 Cor. 9:1; Gal. 1:1).

The New Testament uses the word "apostle" to refer to a few others as well, such as Barnabas (Acts 14:4, 5); James, the brother of our Lord (1 Cor. 15:7); Silvanas and Timothy (1 Thess. 2:6); and others (Rom. 16:7). Although *apostle* generally means "sent one," the New Testament writers use it in a special sense to refer to the human instruments of Christ's ministry. Two specific qualifications were expected of apostles: they must have been eyewitnesses of Jesus (1 Cor. 9:1), and they must have been witnesses of the resurrection of the Lord (Acts 1:21, 22).

Thus while all Christians may be considered as "sent ones" for the proclamation of the gospel, it is presumptuous and inappropriate for anyone today to appropriate the title "apostle." That unique title was applicable to the New Testament time when the Lord Himself called certain men as His apostles to care for the emerging church.

"This principle bears with equal weight upon a question that has long agitated the Christian world—the question of apostolic succession. Descent from Abraham was proved, not by name and lineage, but by likeness of character. So the apostolic succession rests not upon the transmission of ecclesiastical authority, but upon spiritual relationship. A life actuated by the apostles' spirit, the belief and teaching of the truth they taught, this is the true evidence of apostolic succession."[5] Hence there is no biblical basis for anyone to claim to be an apostle or a successor to the apostles, as does the Roman Catholic Church in claiming that the pope is the successor to Peter.

The second gift is that of prophets. Most of the Bible was written by prophets. The word "prophet" occurs more than 300 times in the Old Testament and some 125 times in the New. Someone has pointed out that the work of a prophet may be described in one or more of three ways—to "foretell" a situation or event; to "for tell," that is, speak as God's representative or agent; or to "forth tell," to proclaim boldly, without compromise or ambiguity. Prophets in the Bible were courageous spokespersons for God.

But God has not limited the gift of prophecy to Bible times. One of the signs of God's church in the last day is that it will have the gift of prophecy (Rev. 12:17; 19:10). It is a gift that we can ignore only at our peril.

Third on our list of gifts is evangelists. Although the noun "evangelist" appears only three times in the New Testament (Eph. 4:11; Acts 21:8; 2 Tim. 4:5), the verb "to evangelize" occurs frequently. Christ's Great Commission obligates every Christian to go and preach and teach. In that sense every Christian is an evangelist, although only some may have received the special gift of evangelistic preaching and persuasion. Not all are called to be a Moody or a Spurgeon or a Billy Graham or an H.M.S. Richards. But all are called to be witnesses.

I was stranded at an airport, tired and hungry. My flight was delayed indefinitely. After an hour of waiting I went to the airport restaurant and ordered a simple meal. The waiter politely informed me that it would take 15 minutes to get the food ready. "That's fine," I assured him. Within two minutes he was back again, this time with a pamphlet in his hand. "Perhaps you would like to read this while you wait." The pamphlet was on who Jesus is, and was issued by the Seventh-day Adventist publishing house in Manila.

The time came to check in my luggage. The airline clerk profusely apologized for the delay. She checked my luggage, gave me my boarding pass, and, just as I was leaving, handed me a magazine. "Something to read while you wait," she said with a smile. *A Signs of the Times,* 9 months old.

"Where are you coming from?" I was startled from my nap some

30,000 feet in the air. An elderly gentleman had moved from his seat and had taken a vacant one next to me.

"India," I told him.

Full of questions about India, he showed a great deal of enthusiasm. A few minutes later he gave me a card and suggested that I should enroll in a correspondence school. "You would find in Jesus your best friend, as you get to know Him," he insisted. I told him I was only visiting the Philippines. "Never mind," the elderly man smiled again. "We have a branch in India, and I will ask them to mail the lessons to you." He was persistent in enrolling me in the Voice of Prophecy.

Within a matter of just an hour, three Adventists had shared their faith with me. That is evangelism.

Then Paul's list of gifts names pastors and teachers. The phrase could be translated "pastors who are teachers." All pastors are teachers, for they not only teach and nurture their congregation in the Word of God; they also care for God's people pastorally, shepherding them through their spiritual health. A congregation starving for God's Word will wither and die. That is one of the great dangers facing today's body of Christ, including the Adventist Church.

Seventh-day Adventists are foremost in evangelism. But take a realistic look. Visit some of those areas where the membership has grown by leaps and bounds. On any given Sabbath, would you find a majority, or even 50 percent, of those newly baptized in the pews of a church? Has stewardship gone up proportionately? Honest answers can be quite revealing. What is lacking is nurture. The evangelist's adventure and joy often become the pastor's nightmare and grief. So here's one gift, that of pastoring and teaching, for which everyone needs to pray.

These four gifts are not the only ones given to the church. Paul mentions several more in Romans 12:6-8 and 1 Corinthians 12:28-31, such as ministry, exhortation, liberal giving, leadership, mercy, cheerfulness, miracles, healings, helps, administration, speaking in tongues, and above all, love. The gifts vary; all members will not receive the same gift, although there are certain gifts that should be part of all Christians, such as mercy, cheerfulness, helps, and love. But more than the debate as to what gift we have in comparison to what other Christians have, the most important issue is to discover our own gift. And we should ask the question Why has God given us these spiritual gifts?

Why Spiritual Gifts? (Ephesians 4:12-16)

Ephesians 4:12 lists two reasons that gifts are given to the church: "the equipping of the saints for the work of ministry" and "the edifying of the body of Christ."

The Greek for "equipping" is *katartismon,* which means "to put right," such as mending a torn net (Matt. 4:21) or in medical practice setting a broken bone. By nature there is much brokenness and tornness among us: Jews and Greeks, male and female, educated and illiterate, White and Black, to name a few. With such divisions we cannot be prepared for the work of the ministry. So the apostle tenderly pleads that we let the Spirit and His various gifts work upon us, fix our brokenness, mend our tornness, and create unity by destroying all walls of division so that we are fully equipped for God's work.

Further, the apostle projects that this work of "equipping" and "edifying" is not a temporary one. It is an ongoing one till we all attain "the measure of the stature of the fullness of Christ" (Eph. 4:13). Coming to Christ, experiencing His forgiveness and salvation, being part of the unity of the family of God, and being equipped for His ministry are not enough. Christians must grow in Christ. Paul lists five essentials of such growth (verses 14-16).

Christian growth is continuous. Christian maturity is not a goal that one achieves suddenly. It is the goal toward which we journey. Every day is a day of discovery; every day we find an area in which we need to grow. "Man may grow up into Christ, his living head. It is not the work of a moment, but that of a lifetime. By growing daily in the divine life, he will not attain to the full stature of a perfect man in Christ until his probation ceases. The growing is a continuous work."[6]

Christian growth is moving from childhood to adulthood. God wants us to be childlike, but not childish. He expects us to put away "childish things" (1 Cor. 13:11) and assert the maturity of adulthood with which one can make a distinction between the spiritual and the worldly and take solid food instead of milk (1 Cor. 3:2).

Christian growth is standing firm. To remain in infancy and not grow into mature adulthood is one of the great dangers, dare we say Satan's traps, facing Christians. Paul defines that danger by saying that those who remain in faith's infancy are "tossed to and fro and carried about with every wind of doctrine, by the trickery of men, in the cunning craftiness of deceitful plotting" (Eph. 4:14).

The antidote for such behavior is steady growth in truth and doctrine.

Truth and doctrine cannot come unless one is committed to Jesus, who Himself is the truth. We must turn to the one sure source in which He has revealed that truth. No Christian can mature or grow without continual study of God's Word and a meaningful prayer life. Prayer and Bible study are essential to maturity in Christian life. Mature Christians must be grounded in God's Word so that when "trickery," "craftiness," and "plotting" confront us, they may stand firm on God's testimony (Isa. 8:20).

Christian growth is "speaking the truth in love" (Eph. 4:15). Literally, it is doing the truth. And doing it in love. As Stott says, "truth becomes hard if it is not softened by love; love becomes soft if it is not strengthened by truth."[7]

Christian growth is growing in community, with the recognition that Christ is head (verses 15, 16). No part of the body can function without a permanent and abiding link with the head. The head supplies the power and controls the functions of each body part to perform its assigned function. All the parts must function in unity and harmony. Likewise, unless Christ and His claims permeate every member of the church body, unless Christ takes control of the mind and the function of the corporate body of believers, the growth and maturity of both the individual and the community stand in danger.

Growing up in Christ will result in being like Christ.

---

[1] *The Seventh-day Adventist Bible Commentary,* Ellen G. White Comments, vol. 6, p. 1117.

[2] E. G. White, *Testimonies for the Church,* vol. 1, p. 416.

[3] W. Barclay, *The Letter to the Galatians and the Ephesians,* p. 140.

[4] White, *Testimonies for the Church,* vol. 8, p. 170.

[5] White, *The Desire of Ages,* p. 467.

[6] White, *Testimonies for the Church,* vol. 4, p. 367.

[7] John R. W. Stott, *The Message of Ephesians: God's New Society* (Downers Grove, Ill.: InterVarsity Press, 1979), p. 172.

CHAPTER 9

Living the New Life

Ephesians 4:17-32

Having laid out the initial road map of Christian life (Eph. 4:1-16), Paul proceeds to describe that life as a radical transformation that rejects old values and adopts a totally new lifestyle—in thought, character, values, relationships, and motives. The new life is passing from death to life. It is a change of owners—from Satan to Christ. Paul presents this new life in terms of three steps: putting off the old, putting on the new, and living under new control.

The New Life: Put Off the Old (Ephesians 4:17-23)

The Christian life begins with a clean and clear break from the past. The apostle's charge is unmistakable: "Put off . . . the old man" and "no longer walk as the rest of the Gentiles walk" (Eph. 4:22, 17). The charge is not some abstract theory but a call to action that affects one's total life—thoughts, character, personality, lifestyle. Paul is quite serious about the command. "So I tell you this," he says, "and insist on it in the Lord" (verse 17, NIV). Paul invokes the authority of the Lord and insists that the Christian life must stand in absolute contrast to the life of the Gentiles.

What was the life of the Gentiles like? What was life like before coming to Christ? Paul clusters the characteristics of a Christless life in one phrase: "the futility of [the] mind" (verse 17). The apostle does not deny the intellectual skills of a person without Christ. Indeed, from times before the apostle till now, intellectual greatness, logical thinking, rational arguments, philosophical quest, ethical loftiness, scientific advance, and historical perseverance have characterized human thought.

Yes, we owe much to the human mind. Its persistent quest to understand the unknown and its ability to analyze, synthesize, and preserve human knowledge have been baffling indeed. Who could deny the power of Plato, the persistence of Galileo, the virtuosity of Beethoven, the brilliance of Shakespeare, the creativity of Michaelangelo, the genius of Einstein, or the compassion of Gandhi?

Paul is not saying that these skills and abilities of the human mind are futile. He does say that the moral and spiritual depravity of the mind as seen in its opposition, ignorance, or indifference to the Creator's intentions and goals is futile. He is referring to the degeneracy of the mind (Rom. 1:21) when it rejects God's true revelation and gets into forbidden zones of its own making. It creates "self" as its own god; it denies the presence of sin. It leads humans to live as though God does not exist, as though there is no such thing as a moral and spiritual norm to which human life is held responsible by its Creator.

Such a depraved mind lives in moral and spiritual darkness. Under that kind of mind "the "understanding is darkened, being alienated from the life of God" (Eph. 4:18). Darkened understanding leads to darkened behavior, and darkened behavior makes no distinction between good and evil. The result is "blindness of [the] heart," "lewdness," "uncleanness," and "greediness" (verses 18, 19). In short, the futility of the mind.

The futile mind is what is behind "the old man which grows corrupt according to the deceitful lusts" (verse 22). The Christian calling, therefore, is to crucify the old. The crucifixion of the old self (Gal. 2:20) is essential for "[putting] on the new man" (Eph. 4:24). Death of the old self comes as a result of the conversion experience, but it is an experience that must be guarded carefully, prayerfully, every day. For crucifixion is a slow death. Our only safeguard is to live continually under God's grace, seek His power, and abide in His love.

This act of putting off the old and putting on the new is not one that humans can accomplish on their own. It comes only as a result of the work of Christ in transforming us from the old into the new. This transformation is a result of the truth that is in Jesus (verse 21). This is the only time Paul uses the name "Jesus" in this chapter. His usage here is not incidental. The apostle wants the believers to know that the historic Jesus—the incarnate, the crucified, the risen, and the ascended one—is not a myth. He is real. He lived in our midst. He died for us. He rose again. He ascended to His Father.

This incarnate Jesus is also the incarnate Truth. He said of Himself, "I am the way, the truth, and the life. No one comes to the Father except through Me" (John 14:6). A divine exclusiveness has foreordained that only through Jesus can one receive redemption from sin. "Nor is there salvation in any other, for there is no other name under heaven given among men by which we must be saved" (Acts 4:12).

What is the truth in Jesus that leads us from the old to the new? What is it that Jesus has that no one else has? Simply this: He is God who took on human flesh and suffered for us. "In the beginning was the Word, and the Word was with God, and the Word was God. He was in the beginning with God. All things were made through Him, and without Him nothing was made that was made. In Him was life, and the life was the light of men. . . . And the Word became flesh and dwelt among us, and we beheld His glory, the glory as of the only begotten of the Father, full of grace and truth" (John 1:1-14). Truth that Jesus is God and at the same time God incarnate in human flesh makes Him eligible to be our Savior. Take away His divinity, and He does not have the authority to save. Take away His humanity, and He does not have the means of an example in obedience and the substitutionary role for our sin.

Ellen White speaks of the truth that Christ is our Savior in words that are both poetic and theologically insightful: "By His life and His death, Christ has achieved even more than recovery from the ruin wrought through sin. It was Satan's purpose to bring about an eternal separation between God and man; but in Christ we become more closely united to God than if we had never fallen. In taking our nature, the Savior has bound Himself to humanity by a tie that is never to be broken. Through the eternal ages He is linked with us."[1]

That is the core truth in Jesus: the crucified and risen Savior. When this truth becomes part of our life—the controlling part, the center and focus of our thought, action, and being—then we have indeed put off the old man and put on the new man. Putting on the new means "to grasp the new creation which he [Christ] has made possible, and the entirely new life which results from it. It is nothing less than putting off our old humanity like a rotten garment and putting on like clean clothing the new humanity created in God's image."[2]

The New Life: Put on the New (Ephesians 4:23-29)

Tom was young and energetic, and loved soccer. As a teenager he was champion of his high school soccer team. He could kick the ball so high and so far that he simply dazzled the spectators. He was a hero, a picture of physical strength. But the year he turned 18 tragedy struck. Suddenly he found himself weak, unable to wake up on time, powerless to kick the ball. Even walking became strenuous and tiresome. His parents took him to the best of doctors. His classmates and teachers held long prayer sessions. Arriving at the diagnosis drained out even the little energy Tom had left. He had a dreaded disease, leukemia.

Among the many treatments the doctors tried was blood transfusion. All his blood had to be drained out and new blood transfused. The old must go, the new must come in. The process was a lengthy one, and yet there was no assurance that Tom would be normal again.

That's a tragedy of physical life. The Bible attests that in spiritual life also we are afflicted with a tragic diagnosis of depravity—the result of which is sure and certain death. When sin separates the human from God, the separation is eternal. But there is a way out. We must undergo a transfusion: we must drain out the old from our system and let the Divine Physician transfuse us with the new. "The blood of Jesus Christ His Son cleanses us from all sin" (1 John 1:7). This transfusion creates a new person.

Paul's argument for the new life is clear. Putting off the old is not enough. Jesus told the parable of a man who swept and cleaned his life and was freed from an evil spirit that possessed him. But later seven spirits entered him. He had left his life empty, with nothing to take the place of the one evil spirit (Matt. 12:43-45).

Christianity is not a life of negatives. It is a life of positives. It calls for the believer to rise to a higher ground of moral and spiritual living and accountability. The apostle urges, "Be renewed in the spirit of your mind. . . . Put on the new man" (Eph. 4:23, 24). If the life of the old man was characterized by a "futile" mind, the life of the new man is distinguished by a renewed mind. "Do not be conformed to this world," Paul wrote to the Romans, "but be ye transformed by the renewing of your mind" (Rom. 12:2).

The renewal of the mind is not an exercise in intellectual gymnastics. It is a shift of values and practices. It is moving from darkness to light. It is accepting Christ as the sole center and motivator of life and all its activities. "The soul that is yielded to Christ becomes His own fortress, which He holds in a revolted world, and He intends that no authority shall be known in it but His own. A soul thus kept in possession by the heavenly agencies is impregnable to the assaults of Satan."[3]

Observe from the chart below a few of the contrasts between the old man and the new:

THE OLD MAN	THE NEW MAN
futile mind	renewed mind
alienated from God	created according to God
darkened and ignorant	taught in Jesus
unclean and greedy	righteous and holy
corrupt	true
therefore, put off	**therefore, put on**

Putting on the new man demands a total renunciation of the old and the establishment of a new relation with Christ. The new life is "created according to God, in true righteousness and holiness" (Eph. 4:24). Consequently the new life takes on a radically different orientation. The apostle mentions four lifestyle changes:

First, "[put] away lying , . . . speak the truth" (verse 25). Why does the apostle place this injunction at the forefront? Even atheists and non-Christians frown upon lying. Lying is a social anathema throughout society. What, then, is Paul's burden against lying? Could Paul possibly have in mind what he wrote in the Epistle to the Romans about the ungodly? They "exchanged the truth of God for the lie, and worshiped and served the creature rather than the Creator, who is blessed forever" (Rom. 1:25).

Here is the larger portrayal of a life of lying: exchanging the truth of God for the lie of idolatry. The new life in Christ has no place whatsoever for the lie of idolatry in any form—be it the idol of materialism, education, wealth, social status, or whatever that takes the place of God. Paul says the new man will put away all such pretensions and presumptions and will seek truth only.

In addition to this larger picture, Paul is also mindful of truthfulness in all of life's activities. Can a Christian be a used-car salesperson and still be trusted in the community? Can a teacher be so conscientious and consistent that students will be convinced of her fairness and justness even if they get a poor grade? Can a preacher speak against sin and the congregation will hear, not his words, but the Word of God? Transparency and honesty must ever be a Christian's mark of distinction.

Second, "be angry, and do not sin" (Eph. 4:26). Some would consider all anger as sinful, but Christian ethics holds that there is such a thing as rightful anger. Anger per se is not wrong. It can be good or evil, depending on its motivation and purpose.

The supreme example of such righteous anger is found in our Lord's ministry. When a crowd wondered whether Jesus would heal a man with withered hands, He "looked around at them with anger, being grieved by the hardness of their hearts" (Mark 3:5). Then He healed the man. When the Temple had been turned into a marketplace for cheating and self-gratification, in righteous indignation Jesus drove out the money changers and the traders (John 2:15). That is justifiable anger—it is directed toward the deed, not the person.

Wherever religion puts on the cloak of hypocrisy, wherever poverty and injustice dehumanize a person, wherever there is duty without dignity, existence without hope, religion without love, the Christian must show concern, even be angry. What would the world have been like today without Paul's anger against the Galatian heresy, without Luther's revolt against the practice of indulgences, without Wilberforce's anger against child labor, Carey's wrath against widow burning, Lincoln's anger against slavery?

Yes, righteous anger is very much needed in the Christian life. But it must not turn to bitterness, hatred, and resentment in personal relationships. Hence Paul's warning is timely: " 'Be angry, and do not sin': do not let the sun go down on your wrath, nor give place to the devil" (Eph. 4:26, 27).

Anger that is self-serving, debasing to others, selfish and vindictive, abusive and destructive to another person's selfhood and dignity (for example, spousal abuse), is sin, and has no place in the new life of the Christian. We sin when our anger turns to loss of self-control. In any kind of anger—justified or vindictive—the Christian is not to sin. "Do not let the sun go down on your wrath" is the apostle's admonition.

Edwin Stanton, Lincoln's secretary of war, once was accused by a major general of showing favoritism. Stanton was livid with anger and complained to Lincoln. The president listened to the story and advised Stanton to write a strong letter to the general. Stanton did, with words as sharp as he could muster. He showed the letter to the president, who read it and asked Stanton, "What are you going to do now?"

Stanton was taken aback by the strange query. "I am going to mail it, of course," he said.

Lincoln replied, "No; don't do that. Put it in the stove. That's what I do when someone angers me. I write down all my feelings and read it, and that lets my anger off. I then burn the letter and write a new one." Perhaps that is a good way to settle anger before the sun goes down.

Third, "steal no longer, but . . . work" (Eph. 4:28). Stealing is not acceptable in any normal society, but the apostle makes it the Christian's duty to refrain from it. Stop stealing, he says. Steal not one's possessions. Steal not one's character. Steal not your neighbor's reputation by vain gossip. Steal not your employer's time or product. Steal not another's idea. In our age of computers the admonition would be: Steal no program or music or design.

Christian ethics, therefore, is comprehensive. It includes the particular and the general, the monetary and the relational, the written and the spoken word, the living and the relating, work and worship, and giving and receiving. Let no thieving enter any areas of life, for we are called to live in perfect harmony.

The apostle's admonition goes beyond the negative of "do not steal"; he adds, "Work." Work hard, honestly, diligently. Paul's new man is not just a practitioner of the Protestant work ethic but one who takes honesty and truthfulness as a basic virtue of the new Christian life, an underlying principle of human relations.

Paul's philosophy of work has some lessons for us to learn.The new person in Christ should "labor, working with his hands what is good, that he may have something to give him who has need" (verse 28). All work, honestly done for honorable ends, is to be pursued with diligence. Jesus was a carpenter. Paul was a tentmaker. Peter, John, and James were fishermen. Matthew was a tax collector. Amos was a gatherer of sycamore fruits. Moses was a shepherd. Honest work has meaning and dignity.

Fourth, speak truthfully. "Let no corrupt word proceed out of your mouth, but what is good for necessary edification, that it may impart grace to the hearers" (verse 29). Words are powerful tools. They can build or destroy a person. They can spread encouragement, or they can be vicious tools of malice and gossip. The apostle counsels the new person in Christ to guard the tongue; words should edify. The Christian's speech should give no place to gossip and slander (James 5:12). It must be uplifting and noble. It must impart grace to the sinner, love to the lonely, and peace to the suffering.

"I say to you," warned Jesus, "that for every idle word men may speak, they will give account of it in the day of judgment. For by your words you will be justified, and by your words you will be condemned" (Matt. 12:36, 37).

The Rotary Club International has a four-way test that all its members accept as their guide in speaking: "Is it the truth? Is it fair to all concerned? Will it build goodwill and better fellowship? Will it be beneficial to all concerned?" A great formula! But should we who belong to the body of Christ have any less a guide? Indeed, Isaiah's messianic exclamation should become the daily objective of our speech: "The Lord God has given Me the tongue of the learned, that I should know how to speak a word in season to him who is weary" (Isa. 50:4).

The New Life: Under New Control (Ephesians 4:30-32)

The life in Christ is life under the guidance and control of the "Holy Spirit of God, by whom you were sealed for the day of redemption" (Eph. 4:30). The Spirit is the agent of the new life. He is the teacher, the comforter, the third person of the Godhead, through whom Christ indwells (John 14:16-26).

On his first visit with Christians in Ephesus, Paul asked, "Did you receive the Holy Spirit when you believed?" They gave a startling response: "We have not so much as heard whether there is a Holy Spirit." After teaching them about the Holy Spirit, the apostle rebaptized them and laid his hands on them. Then "the Holy Spirit came upon them, and they spoke with tongues and prophesied" (Acts 19:1-6).

That experience must have had a profound and deep impact on the church at Ephesus. The apostle speaks about the Holy Spirit and His role in the life of the church at least 13 times in this Epistle. To note just a few: Ephesians 2:18 speaks about the common access that Gentiles and Jews have to God through the ministry of the Holy Spirit; Ephesians 3:16 speaks of the indwelling of the Spirit that provides strength for the inner self of the Christian; Ephesians 5:9 speaks of the cluster of the fruit of the Spirit; Ephesians 6:17 defines the Word of God as the sword of the Spirit.

In Ephesians 4:30 Paul speaks of the Holy Spirit as the one who seals us for the day of redemption. The apostle has already spoken of this special ministry of the Holy Spirit: "Having believed, you were sealed with the Holy Spirit of promise, who is the guarantee of our inheritance until the redemption of the purchased possession" (Eph. 1:13, 14). Herein we have our assurance for the present and our hope for the future. The assurance is that we are sealed as God's property, redeemed by the blood of His Son. Nothing can snatch us from God's hold; the only way we can lose is by our own decision. The hope for the future is in the statement that the Holy Spirit gives us the guarantee that in that day when all things will be gathered together in one unity under God, we will find our place, safe and secure.

Paul clearly places great importance on the role of the Holy Spirit in the life of the Christian and the congregation. Hence his plea: "Do not grieve the Holy Spirit of God" (Eph. 4:30). This is, perhaps, one of the most significant spiritual obligations of a Christian. But how do we grieve the Holy Spirit?

The immediate context gives us a clue. These sins against the community—lying, stealing, anger, revenge, slander, bitterness, lack of kindness and forgiveness—offend the Holy Spirit, who inhabits the body of Christ. Ephesians mentions other ways whereby we grieve the Holy Spirit: when we do not live like God's children (Eph. 1:13); defile our body, which is God's dwelling place (Eph. 2:22); disrupt the unity of the church (Eph. 4:3, 4); return to the life of the old man (verse 22); and give room for Satan by our lifestyle (verses 25-30). Says John MacArthur: "All sin is painful to God, but sin in His children breaks His heart. When His children refuse to change the ways of the old life for the ways of the new, God grieves. The Holy Spirit of God weeps, as it were, when He sees Christians lying instead of speaking the truth, becoming unrighteously rather than righteously angry, stealing instead of sharing, and speaking corrupt instead of uplifting and gracious words."[4]

The admonition "Do not grieve the Holy Spirit" is immediately followed by further "put off, put on" advice. Put off "all bitterness, wrath, anger, clamor, and evil speaking . . . with all malice," and then put on kindness to one another, tenderheartedness, "forgiving one another, even as God in Christ forgave you" (Eph. 4:31, 32).

Christlikeness is the key to the Christian's new life.

---

[1] E. G. White, *The Desire of Ages,* p. 25.

[2] J.R.W. Stott, *The Message of Ephesians,* p. 180.

[3] White, *The Desire of Ages,* p. 324.

[4] John MacArthur, Jr., *The MacArthur New Testament Commentary: Ephesians* (Chicago: Moody Bible Institute, 1986), p. 189.

CHAPTER 10

Principles of the Christian Walk

Ephesians 5:1-20

Paul proceeds in his discourse on the practical demands of Christian life. He devotes the first 20 verses of Ephesians 5 to the principles of the Christian walk, and then applies these principles to relationships in marriage, in the home, and between servants and masters. Verses 1-20 provide four specific principles that should govern the Christian walk: love, purity, light, and wisdom.

Walk in Love (Ephesians 5:1, 2)

The apostle takes the Christian walk to a new height: "Be imitators of God as dear children" (Eph. 5:1). "Be imitators" is not just an ethical appeal. Many people do not know Christ, yet they live ethical lives. Their ethics extend not only to humans but to all living creatures; they would not think of doing anyone harm. A Jainist monk in India walks with a fan in his hand, clearing the path before him lest he step on an ant. There are communities in the world where if you happen to lose something and someone finds it, you are sure to get it back. So a call to an ethical life is not the central issue in our text—although one who imitates God will be a highly ethical person.

Paul says, "Be imitators of God as dear children." It is natural for children to imitate their parents. So, the apostle says, in Christian life imitate God. God loves; so should we. God forgives; so should we. He is holy; therefore we must be holy. God cares for the least of His creatures; so should we care for the less fortunate in our midst. God does not show any partiality; neither should we. God hates sin but loves the sinner, and so should we. The list can go on, but suffice it to say that God's character is the ultimate norm for the Christian. In Christ a new ethic is born. "The Christian love ethic . . . is the result of a love story. The chief actor in that story is God and not man."[1]

The essential difference between Christianity and mere ethics is that

Christians are called "to imitate God" in His supreme act of the Christ event. Just as God loved the human race in its utter depravity and degradation and gave His Son, Jesus Christ, as "an offering and a sacrifice" (verse 2), so we ought to imitate God.

The imitation of God is the imitation of Christ. We are not called to imitate Jesus the good man, Jesus the moral example, Jesus the great teacher, Jesus the definer of history. Such an imitation, good as far as it goes, is not good enough in the Pauline scheme of Christian life. What Paul insists is that we be "imitators of God"—that is to say, "walk in love, as Christ also has loved us and given Himself for us, an offering and a sacrifice to God for a sweet-smelling aroma" (verse 2).

We cannot imitate God unless we are prepared to imitate His love. The one attribute above all others that God would have His children possess is a love like His. Note the word the apostle uses: "imitate." While we may never reach that perfect stage in which we can love like God loves, we are called to be as close to that as possible through His divine grace. Even that imitation is not of our own; it is a gift of God to those who abide in Him.

How do we imitate God? How do we reflect the image of Christ? The answer is: "Walk in love, as Christ has loved us and given Himself for us." Three characteristics of that love stand out.

First, Christ's love was selfless. His love was agape love—a love that seeks the good of the other person without regard to self. This love is not what we know as affection. We are affectionate to our children, our siblings, our parents, and perhaps even to our friends and neighbors. They have some link between us. There is some likable quality about them, something that is attractive, and so we show affection. And we expect, or hope, that they will show affection toward us. In filial affection, in friendship, in romantic love, there is usually something in it for everyone. But that is not the way Christ loves. Agape is loving the unlovable, the undeserving, the rebellious. "God demonstrates His own love toward us, in that while we were still sinners, Christ died for us" (Rom. 5:8). Not only that, God loves us enough to bring us to His fold as His sons and daughters, and He never gives up on us. He continues to love us when we fail Him, when we forget Him, when we disobey Him, and even when we forsake Him. That is the kind of unselfish love we are called to display on our Christian walk.

Second, Christ's love was sacrificial. The apostle points out that Christ had "loved us and given Himself for us an offering and sacrifice to God for a sweet-smelling aroma" (Eph. 5:2). Paul applies the phrase "sweet-smelling aroma" to the offering and sacrificial love of Christ. The sacrifice of

Jesus was well pleasing to God in that it fulfilled His plan of redemption. Jesus could have refused to go through the agony of Gethsemane and the cross, but His love for the fallen race was so complete and His obedience to God's will so unreserved that He gave Himself. That was Christ's walk of love.

The cross not only creates the Christian community but also reveals the basis of life in that community. That basis is unconditional, sacrificial love; it raises no question about color or caste, ethnic origin or tribal allegiance, nationality or living status, gender or genealogy. Just as God's love led Jesus to lay down His life for all, so should Christian love prepare us for the ultimate sacrifice. "By this we know love, because He laid down His life for us. And we also ought to lay down our lives for the brethren" (1 John 3:16).

History reveals such sacrifice in shining moments here and there, such as during the persecution of the early church and in our own times. But history also records, to our everlasting shame, the impotence of many Christians to stand up against slavery, racism, the Holocaust, ethnic cleansing, the caste system—exploitation of human beings in whatever form. But we need not wait for some big moral issue to demonstrate our love. God's love must be shown here and now. "True religion is the imitation of Christ. Those who follow Christ will deny self, take up the cross, and walk in His footsteps. Following Christ means obedience to all His commandments. . . . Copy Jesus, full of love and tenderness and compassion."[2]

Third, Christ's love is reconciling. Every Christian activity comes under the scrutiny of this ultimate test: Does it reflect the love that caused Jesus to go to the cross? We may say we have the truth. We may claim we are children of light. We may insist we do not belong to the world. All these assertions mean nothing unless they are reflected in a life of love that reaches out to others in reconciliation. "It is the duty of all to learn of Christ, to walk humbly in the self-denying path in which the Majesty of heaven trod. The whole Christian life should be one of self-denial."[3]

Walk in Purity (Ephesians 5:3-7)

The apostle turns from the topic of self-sacrifice, which is pleasing to God, to self-indulgence, which is absolutely repugnant to Him. He names a series of vices that should have no place in the Christian life: "Fornication and all uncleanness or covetousness, let it not even be named among you, as is fitting for saints; neither filthiness, nor foolish talking, nor coarse jesting, which are not fitting, but rather giving of thanks. For this you know, that no fornicator, unclean person, nor covetous man, who is an idolater, has any inheritance in the kingdom of Christ and God" (Eph. 5:3-5).

Paul expresses his horror at these vices: "Let it not even be named among you"—let it not even be a mere joke in your conversation. Anyone who so indulges does not have "any inheritance in the kingdom of Christ and God."

The Greek words for "fornication" (*porneia*) and "impurity" (*akatharsia*) cover every kind of sexual sin. From *porneia* we get the word "pornography," a sickness of mind and body, an indulgence so easily available in our times through the printed page or a click of a computer mouse or a flick of a cable remote. Easy access and anonymity have made this sin available to many, from children to seniors, from custodians of the law to the clergy. Pornography is a deadly addiction: the more one indulges, the deeper one gets into it.

To these sexual sins Paul adds covetousness—a reference to the tenth commandment. In all, Paul talks about sexual perversions and immorality that were common indulgences in Ephesus, a city that fostered the cult of Diana, famous for its temple prostitution. To the apostle these are not just grievous; they disqualify one from the kingdom of God.

It is an awful commentary on current society that its entertainment and communication media glory in sex and its perversions, and make those practices tolerable and even a matter of levity. Even more awful is that authorities—political, legal, clergical, who should stand for principles of moral uprightness—advocate tolerance and even acceptance of such practices. Our Broadways and Hollywoods churn out trash that makes nought of the commandments. The beauty and the dignity of the human body, conceived in God's mind and created by His own hand, become prey to lustful passion and violent mutilation. The apostle has nothing but condemnation for all such sin and perversion. "Don't even talk about such shameful things," he says.

The apostle condemns also vain words. "Let no one deceive you with empty words, for because of these things the wrath of God comes upon the sons of disobedience" (verse 6). What are the empty words with which God's people may be deceived? In Paul's time there was the dangerous doctrine of Gnosticism, which was built on a body-spirit dichotomy—body (or matter) is evil, and spirit is good. Salvation has to do with liberating only the spirit. Things pertaining to the body were of no significance, and so it did not matter what one did with the body. Thus there was no such thing as bodily or sexual sin. That is one kind of empty talk that Paul warns Ephesians to be cautious about.

Another kind of empty talk has to do with a misunderstanding of grace. God's grace is sufficient to forgive all sins. So some people advocate going on sinning, "for God's grace can wipe out every sin." The gospel speaks about the power of grace and the freedom it brings in the life of a sinner, but it never speaks about a situation that permits licentiousness or minimizes the deadliness of sin.

God's grace provides both a privilege and a responsibility. The privilege is that God bestows upon us His free grace and forgives our sins. It is a responsibility in that once sin is forgiven we are expected to walk in the way of obedience and sin no more. No one states this better than Paul himself: "What shall we say, then? Shall we go on sinning so that grace may increase? By no means! We died to sin; how can we live in it any longer?" (Rom. 6:1, 2, NIV). Writes William Barclay: "The gravest disservice any man can do to a fellow man is to make him think lightly of sin. Paul pleaded with his converts not to be deceived with empty words which took the horror from the idea of sin."[4]

Walk in Light (Ephesians 5:8-14)

From "walking in love" and "walking in purity" we now come to the third great principle, "Walk in light." The gospel is essentially a movement from darkness to light—from the darkness of sin to the light of salvation; from the darkness of alienation to the light of Christ's fellowship; from the darkness of evil to the light of "the gospel of the glory of Christ" (2 Cor. 4:4); from the kingdom of the prince of darkness to the kingdom of the One who said, "I am the light of the world" (John 8:12).

This transition from darkness to light places believers in a position of great privilege and responsibility. The light refers to more than intellectual truth. In addition to intellectual understanding that drives out the darkness, believers have the spiritual light that brings deliverance from the works of Satan (verses 38, 41, 44), the domain and authority of Satan (Col. 1:12; Eph. 6:12), the wrath of God reserved for children of darkness (Eph. 5:6; 2:3), and from the ultimate penalty of death (Rom. 6:23; 2 Peter 2:17).

Being in this spiritual light, we are to walk in it. That walk is part of imitating God, who is the eternal light. How do we walk in the light? Not in the sense of being enlightened, but in the sense of the whole being—mind, body, and spirit—coming under the continuing influence and control of the One who is light, in whom there is "no darkness at all" (1 John 1:5). The apostle elaborates this further with a series of musts in a Christian life. First, practice "the fruit of the Spirit . . . goodness, righteousness, and truth" (Eph. 5:9). The fruit of the Spirit points to a high moral and spiritual ground of living for God. Walking in light, the Christian life is an open book for all to see what the glory of God has accomplished where once was darkness.

Second, walking in light is walking according to "what is acceptable to the Lord" (verse 10). We find out what is acceptable to God by keeping close to Him through His Word and through prayer.

Third, "have no fellowship with the unfruitful works of darkness, but rather expose them" (verse 11). An old Indian adage says that light is absence of darkness, and darkness is absence of light. Whatever that may mean, one thing is true—light and darkness cannot coexist. As children of light Christians must so live that they expose the evils of darkness. We must be known in voice and action for our stand against evil's every manifestation. Not only will we have no "fellowship" with works of darkness; we will expose through our life and character the futility of the works of darkness. "Such a character is not the result of accident; it is not due to special favors or endowments of Providence. A noble character is the result of self-discipline, of the subjection of the lower to the higher nature—the surrender of self for the service of love to God and man."[5]

Walk in Wisdom (Ephesians 5:15-20)

Paul concludes his discussion of the Christian walk with a fourth principle. Walk in love, walk in purity, walk in light, and now walk "not as fools but as wise" (Eph. 5:15). Paul defines this wisdom in four components, all equally important.

First, to walk wisely to is to "walk circumspectly" (verse 15). As the Revised Standard Version states: "Look carefully then how you walk." Look. Walk. Christians must look where they are going. They live in this world, but their destination is elsewhere. That journey of faith requires great care and watchfulness. Keep your eyes focused on the path ahead. The road is narrow (Matt. 7:14); it may be full of hurdles, potholes, or other dangers. The road also has signposts and directions; if you miss a sign, you may go off course. You must always keep the direction and the condition of the road in focus.

When I was in the eighth grade, we had to take state-controlled public examinations that were set and corrected by strangers in some distant part of the state. It was essential that we pass these examinations with high scores in order to get into high school. Our school had arranged special times at night for us to study in the school, as most of our homes were small and did not have electricity. For some three months prior to the examinations, after supper several of us would walk to the school, about a mile away. The road was unpaved and had bushes on either side. As I left home each night my father would say, "Watch your steps. Look where you are going."

About 15 of us boys would walk together, two or three abreast. One night I felt something like a thorn prick on my left foot. Within minutes I was in pain. We were almost at the school, and my friends carried me in. My left foot and leg swelled. A cobra had bitten me. When he heard the word, my father rushed to the school. He did not have much of an education, but he knew some first aid. With a sharp blade he cut the place where the snake's two teeth marks were visible, and sucked and spat out the poison. Several men took turns carrying me to a hospital some two miles away. Everything turned out OK, but my leg remained swollen for some months.

The spiritual road that we are called to walk has grave pitfalls. The darkness holds dangers, and the old serpent has more than one trap along the way. So Paul's admonition is a timely one: Look carefully; don't be careless like the unwise; walk wisely. Remember the words of the psalmist, "Your word is a lamp to my feet and a light to my path" (Ps. 119:105).

Second, to walk wisely is to redeem time, because the days are evil (Eph. 5:15). The Greek for "time" here is not *chronos* but *kairos*. *Chronos* refers to what we measure by a clock—hours, minutes, and seconds. *Kairos* is a period allotted for a particular purpose. God in His sovereign will has given to each of us *kairos*. It's a time period the boundary of which is set by His will; we know we have this time, but we do not know when we'll lose it. It's not in our hands, and therefore we need to make "the most of the time" (verse 16, RSV). Or as the New International Version has it, make the "most of every opportunity."

To live with a sense that time is borrowed is part of the Christian's responsibility. Moreover, "the days are evil" (verse 16) and call for God's intervention to establish the new age. How important it is, therefore, that the Christian make good use of every opportunity.

Jonathan Edwards, a great preacher of the eighteenth century, wrote this resolution on his twentieth birthday: "Resolved: Never to lose one moment of time, but to improve it in the most profitable way I possibly can." To live as a Christian is to live with a sense of time. A present life and an eschatological hope are the parenthesis within which we are called to live.

Third, to walk wisely is to "understand what the will of the Lord is" (verse 17). Nothing is more important than to discover the will of God for one's life and to submit to it. At the young age of 12 Jesus knew the will of God and placed it above His love for His parents. He asked them, "Did you not know that I must be about My Father's business?" (Luke 2:49).

Later, faced with the agony and the uncertainty of Gethsemane and the cross, Jesus again sought the will of God: "O My Father, if it is possible, let this cup pass from Me; nevertheless, not as I will, but as You will" (Matt. 26:39).

God's basic will for us is revealed in Scripture. Here we find His perfect and unerring guidance as to what we should do and how we should do it. It is God's will that we choose to honor Him, to glorify Him, and to be in harmony with His Word.

But how do we find His will for us in particular situations, such as Whom should I marry? What educational career should I choose? What business should I go into? A Christian has a hundred decisions to make each day. How does one make such decisions in harmony with God's will? First, turn to the Scriptures, and there you will hear God's will. Second, pray. Take your request earnestly before God and await His guidance. Remember that God's ultimate will is our sanctification (1 Thess. 4:3); anything that hinders that objective cannot be the will of God.

Fourth, to be wise is to "be filled with the Spirit" (Eph. 5:18). To be filled with the Spirit is the highest mark of a person's spiritual life. Paul places it in contrast to what cannot be the best in a person's life: "Do not be drunk with wine" (verse 18). Drinking has no role in the Christian life. Alcohol has power to enslave, to depress, and to demolish one's self-dignity. It also causes one to relate poorly with others. The apostle warns against the folly of becoming a slave to alcohol.

Instead, the Christian life should be filled with the Spirit. The Spirit gives power to live in fellowship, worship, gratitude, and submission (verses 19-21). In using the phrases "drunk with wine" and "filled with the Spirit," the apostle raises a vital question in life: under whose control are we as Christians—the Holy Spirit's or someone else's? "The focus of Paul's words here is not so much the prohibition against drunkenness, for the believers probably already understood that, but his urging that they continually be filled by and live in the Spirit. When a person is drunk, everyone can tell. His or her actions make it obvious. In like manner, our lives should be so completely under the Spirit's control that our actions and words show beyond a doubt that we are filled with the presence of God's Holy Spirit."[6]

---

[1] *The Interpreter's Bible,* vol. 10, p. 705.

[2] *The Seventh-day Adventist Bible Commentary,* Ellen G. White Comments, vol. 7, p. 949.

[3] E. G. White, *Testimonies for the Church,* vol. 7, p. 297.

[4] W. Barclay, *The Letters to the Galatians and the Ephesians,* p. 163.

[5] Ellen G. White, *Education* (Mountain View, Calif.: Pacific Press Pub. Assn., 1903), p. 57.

[6] *Life Application Bible Commentary: Ephesians* (Wheaton, Ill.: Tyndale House Pub., Inc., 1996), p. 109.

CHAPTER 11

Christian Relationships

Ephesians 5:21–6:9

Christianity, in the final analysis, is not a set of doctrines or a series of theological formulations. It is a way of life based on the good news of a redeemed relationship. It is a new creation, founded by the reconciling ministry of Christ on the cross. On the one hand, it links humanity with God; on the other, it bridges the gulf that separates humans from humans, community from community, nation from nation. Christianity is the home that love built, where God reigns supreme and all redeemed members of the human community dwell in harmony and fellowship.

Paul takes this theme of harmony and goodwill and applies it to the Christian's closest human relationship. From Ephesians 5:22 to 6:9 the apostle stresses the powerful impact the gospel should have on three vital areas of life—marital relations, parent-child relations, and relationships at work and business. According to Paul, the gospel is not limited to heaven and heavenly things; it is also about the kitchen and the bedroom, the crib and the school, the workplace and work.

But before we enter into that main study, we need to understand an important principle of submission and authority. "Submitting to one another in the fear of God," begins Paul (Eph. 5:21) as he counsels wives. Paul's conversion from pharisaical Judaism to the Christian gospel was so complete that his understanding of anthropology and sociology was transformed. He could not accept the Jewish position that the Jew was superior to the Gentile, that a man was of more value than a woman, that a free person was worth more than a slave. Nor could he agree with the Roman and Greek arrogance that somehow they stood superior to any other race.

Thus Paul could never think of servility when he speaks of submission. Nor will he, as we will see shortly, describe wives as inferior to their husbands. To Paul, submission is an attitude of humility and a courteous consideration of the other person. Relationships in a redeemed community should be marked with respect for one another. But even for this the apostle places a defining parameter: "in the fear of God," that is, as the NIV translates, "out of reverence for Christ." Just as Christ embraced humility and submission (Phil. 2:5-8) in order to fulfill His Father's will and purpose in bringing about cosmic reconciliation, so should God's children live in humility and submission to one another in order that God's plan may be fulfilled in and through us.

Husband and Wife (Ephesians 5:22-33)

This long passage provides a beautiful testimony regarding the status of Christian marriage. What the apostle wrote was timely and appropriate when he wrote it; it is no less timely today, when the institution of marriage is under attack from all sides. At the time of Paul, Jews, Greeks, and Romans alike had a very poor and narrow opinion of marriage, particularly as to the role of women.

In spite of their heritage of the magnificent story of Creation, Jews had developed a sociology in which women had little worth. It is said that the Orthodox Jew of that time thanked God daily that he was not created a slave, a Gentile, or a female. Divorce for the male Jew was common and easy. All he had to do was write a bill of divorce and hand it to his wife, and there ended the marriage. Grounds for divorce were simple: if she found "no favor in his eyes" or he "found some uncleanness in her" (Deut. 24:1).

Although the Shammai rabbis interpreted this to mean adultery, the more liberal Hillel rabbis gave the phrase a broad latitude—the "no favor" clause could be invoked if the wife put too much salt in the food, did not cover her head when she went out, spoke to another man on the street, said something disrespectful about her parents-in-law, etc. We can imagine which rabbinical tradition prevailed.

The situation in Greek and Roman society was no better. Prostitution was an accepted part of Greek life; it revolved around pagan deities and was practiced freely in temples. A man had a wife in order to produce legitimate children who would inherit his property; he had courtesans and concubines for his pleasure. The Roman society developed its permissiveness to an almost unlimited licentiousness. Seneca, a renowned Roman poet, once wrote that women were married to be divorced, and divorced to be married. Multiple marriages for men and women were not uncommon. Jerome cites an instance in which a woman was married to her twenty-third husband, who himself had been married 20 times before. Such was the sexual debauchery and marital chaos.

Against this background of a society in decay, Jesus affirmed the sacredness of marriage. He spoke against infidelity and flimsy excuses for divorce. He reaffirmed the Old Testament provision that adultery is the only ground for divorce (Matt. 19:9). The apostle further introduced the revolutionary truth that "there is neither Jew nor Greek, there is neither slave nor free, there is neither male nor female; for you are all one in Christ Jesus" (Gal. 3:28). As a result, a new understanding of marriage and the role of husband and wife emerged in the Christian community, which was to affect for the better both the institution of marriage and the social status of women.

However, some female members of the church, in celebration of this new spirit of equality and freedom, decided to take their liberty to the extent of disturbing the mutual love, support, and submission that should characterize the relationship within the Christian home. It is in this context that we should read Paul's admonition for wives to be submissive and for husbands to be loving. Submission does not mean servility. Paul does not consider women as slaves to their husbands, but as equal partners in the sacred institution of marriage. The wife should not revolt against her husband in the name of freedom, but remain supportive and considerate of him. Similarly, the husband must realize that he has no right to suppress his wife, but should instead be loving. The responsibility of love, submission, understanding, and support are mutually recognized principles for preserving the strength and the unity of the home—particularly the Christian home.

The apostle uses four arguments to strengthen his teaching on marriage and the role of its primary partners. **First, the argument of Genesis (Eph. 5:31; Gen. 2:21-24).** Marriage is not a result of human anthropology or sociology. It is part of the creative activity of God. He who created the heavens and the earth also created man and woman and brought them together in the most intimate relationship of marriage. The two beings became one flesh, so that the interests of one became the interests of the other, the concerns and joy of one became the concerns and joys of the other. "Bone of my bones and flesh of my flesh" (Gen. 2:23) is the way Scripture describes the oneness and unity of marriage.

The Creation account further emphasizes the supremacy of love that governs this unity. The husband and wife, in experiencing the one-flesh mystery, shall place priority on their oneness, even to the extent of leaving their parents. Indeed, the relationship between husband and wife shall be so open and intimate that nothing shall be hidden between them. "They were both naked, . . . and were not ashamed" (verse 25). When love is at the basis of a relationship, the question of superiority and inferiority, authority and submission, does not arise.

Second, the argument of Christ and the church. Just as Christ is the head of the church, so is the husband the head of the wife (Eph. 5:23). How did Christ become the head of the church? Paul gives one answer in the last portion of the same verse: "He is the Savior of the body." Christ is the head of the church because He gave Himself as a sacrifice on the cross. By that act He created a community of the redeemed, and for this community He became the head. By the extraordinary sacrifice of Himself, by the inordinate love that He had for the sinners, Christ was able to draw a community of believers to Himself. This community is His body, of which He Himself is the head.

As the head, Christ is the source and has the functional responsibility for the church in all its functions. The church, as the body of Christ, cannot function or even exist without the headship of Christ. Says John Stott: "It is from Christ as head that the body derives its health and grows into maturity. His headship expresses care rather than control, responsibility rather than rule. This truth is endorsed by the surprising addition of the words *and is himself its savior.* The head of the body is the savior of the body; the characteristic of his headship is not so much lordship as saviorhood."[1]

Paul applies this analogy of Christ's headship over the church to marriage. The ideal Christian marriage is one in which the husband sacrifices self-interests; out of his deep love he considers his wife as one flesh with him. Unity, love, fellowship, selflessness, and a spirit of sacrifice mark the marital union. Such perfect union recognizes both the headship of the husband (not in terms of dictatorial authority or male chauvinism but in terms of sacrificial love and creation's ideal) and the submission of the wife (not in terms of servitude but in terms of "preferring one another" as in the Lord). And for both, Christ is the model. In submission the wife does not lose her dignity; in love the husband does not lose his masculinity.

The third point in Paul's discussion regarding marriage is that even as Christ loved the church so should husbands love their wives (Eph. 5:25). Christ's love for the church is unconditional, sacrificial, and unending. It is this commitment of the risen Savior that sanctifies the church, sets that body apart as His own, and preserves it as a glorious, functioning body. When this analogy is applied to Christian marriage, the implications are both enormous and marvelous. In the face of that kind of love, what wife would not be moved to respond in kind and give herself completely to her mate?

The key to understand the obligation of the husband to his wife is found in Christ's sacrificial obligation for His bride, the church (verses 25-28). "Dare I put it like this?" asks Lloyd-Jones. "The Beauty-Specialist will have put his final touch to the church, the massaging will have been so perfect that there will not be a single wrinkle left. She will look young, and in the bloom of youth, with colour in her cheeks, with her skin perfect, without any spots or wrinkles. And she will remain like that forever and for ever."[2]

That's what Jesus as the head of the church does for the church. So should the husband do to the wife as her head. Therefore, anyone who builds a case for male chauvinism out of the word "submissive" should read this verse again and again. Here we don't have a picture of male superiority and female inferiority. Instead we have a portrait of unconditional love: "He who loves his wife loves himself" (verse 28).

The fourth point: just as Christ nourishes and cherishes the church, so should the husband nourish and cherish his wife (verse 29). This relationship between Christ and His church, says Paul, is a "great mystery" (verse 32). Earlier Paul used the word "mystery" to refer to God's great plan for universal reconciliation as one body in Christ (Eph. 1:9) and the Jewish-Gentile unity as one body (Eph. 3:3, 4, 9). Now he uses the word to speak of the unity that exists between Christ and the church (Eph. 5:32)—each time referring to the making of one out of many. Once more before he completes the Epistle he will use the word to speak about the "mystery of the gospel" (Eph. 6:19), indicating that reconciliation that comes through redemption.

Although the apostle does not apply the word "mystery" to the union of husband and wife in marriage, he well could. A theology of marriage relationships cannot be complete without including the mystical unity that ought to exist between husband and wife. The two becoming one flesh is the activity of divine grace. Where that grace is absent, there is discord in marriage. Hence Paul concludes his testament on marriage by a twofold appeal: to the husbands that they love their wives; to wives that they "respect" their husbands (Eph. 5:33).

Parents and Children (Ephesians 6:1-4)

I remember the month I began denominational service, nearly 50 years ago. I stood at a quiet graveside at Karmatar, a sleepy little village 170 miles northwest of Calcutta. That grave held the remains of Dores A. Robinson, the first official leader of the work of the Adventist Church in India. Within five years of his arrival in India he established a school, organized a church, started an orphanage, and initiated a literature program. He also adopted an Indian girl, sending out a symbolic message that the triumph of the gospel is more than individual salvation; it must break down the wall of partition that compartmentalizes a community. It must open wide the doors of the kingdom. Caring for the orphans and the poor was part of his consuming passion as a preacher of the gospel of Jesus Christ.

As Robinson continued his work day after day, with little or no break, a case of smallpox was discovered in the village. The British officers at district headquarters sent word to all foreigners to leave the area and go to the safety of a city. Such winds of death were not uncommon in those days. Many government officials and some missionaries heeded the government's advice. But not Robinson. This was the time his orphaned children and poor villagers needed him the most. So he stayed on and did all he could to help as many as possible. But within a few weeks the shadow of death cast its spell on him. He fell victim to the dreaded disease, and his grave stands as a monument to Christian love and care for the children.

No other religion or ideology has done as much for children as Christianity. William Wilberforce, a devout Christian, ended child labor in England. William Carey, the pioneer of Christian missions, acted to end child marriage and widow burning in India. Today in some rural areas of southern India, female infants are choked or poisoned to death. Christian hospitals and pastors have set up cradles outside their doors to accept unwanted female infants so as to save them from a cruel death.

Roman culture during the time of the apostle Paul had a cruel set of values toward unfortunate children. Barclay quotes the famous Seneca: "We slaughter a fierce ox; we strangle a mad dog; we plunge the knife into sick cattle lest they taint the herd; children who are born weakly and deformed we drown."[3]

It was under such circumstances that Paul wrote to Christian parents and their children in Ephesus, a Roman city. How delighted the children must have been to hear themselves mentioned in a letter from the great apostle. He expects the children to obey their parents, and he gives two reasons for doing so. First, it is right. It is a proper thing for children to obey their parents, and every culture of society expects it. Second, God's moral law demands such obedience. The apostle quotes the fifth commandment (Eph. 6:2, 3) and proclaims it as the basis for children to honor and obey their parents.

Paul's injunction to children to obey their parents has a condition: "in the Lord." The apostle was aware that often parents are not exactly models of God's expectations. If a father tells a child to deliver illegal drugs to a buyer, should the child obey? If a father, to meet his economic needs or support the family, pressures his daughter into prostitution, should the girl follow his directions? The apostle draws the line in three mighty words—"in the Lord." Those words are a guide not only to children's conduct, but to all. The divine will is the unalterable, ever-enduring, ethical norm for all human behavior.

Susannah Wesley, the mother of John and Charles, raised a large family. She had this to say about child raising: "The parent who studies to subdue [self-will] in his child works together with God in the renewing and saving of a soul. The parent who indulges it does the devil's work, makes religion impracticable, salvation unattainable, and does all that in him lies to damn his child, soul and body forever."[4]

Paul's counsel to children carries a corollary responsibility to parents. "And you, fathers, do not provoke your children to wrath, but bring them up in the training and admonition of the Lord" (verse 4). How do parents provoke children to wrath? For one thing, by playing favoritism between siblings. Jacob was a prime example. By his favoritism toward Joseph he built up wrath among his older sons against their brother and, in a way, against himself.

Another thing that provokes resentment in children is parental expectations that may be more than the child can handle. When a parent expects a child to get all A grades when that's beyond the child's ability, the child can get angry or resentful. Comparing one's child with a neighbor's—or worse yet, with a friend of the child's—leads to poor self-worth and eventually to resentment.

Physical abuse of children leaves scars of anger and resentment that may affect the child for a lifetime. Martin Luther once said that it may be OK to "spare the rod and spoil the child," but it is good to leave an apple for the child. In other words, there's a big difference between discipline and abuse.

Another important situation that children resent is hypocrisy and double standards on the part of parents. I think of Martin George, who claimed to be a very religious person and who as a father kept his children in obedience and discipline. Returning home one day, he was met by a deadening silence.

His wife was quiet. His son, Ron, was nowhere to be seen. Martin was curious to know what had happened to the usually joyous home.

Slowly his wife told him what had happened. Ron's teacher had called her earlier. It seemed that Ron had stolen a pencil from another student but when found out he lied about it. Later he admitted his stealing.

Martin was quite upset. What would the community think of him and his family? What would the church think of him? His 7-year-old son had brought a bad name to the family. The sin deserved punishment. So the father called Ron to the stand of justice, took a cane, and gave him four lashes. The little boy cried, and even as he cried the father gave him a lecture. "Why did you steal that pencil? You could have told me that you needed a pencil. I would have brought you as many as you needed from my office."

Little Ron's crying turned into a stare of wonder. In Paul's words, Martin provoked his son to wrath. "Parents who successfully govern their families must first govern themselves. If they would only have pleasant words in their families, they must let their children hear only pleasant words from their lips."[5]

Slaves and Masters (Ephesians 6:5-9)

Slavery is perhaps one of the worst tragedies that sin has wrought on human community. Almost every society in every part of the world has suffered the evils that spring from slavery. Even today this social evil prevails in one form or another. There are countries where slavery exists in the form of indentured labor, where generation after generation live as bonded laborers on the farms of rich and exploitative people. Children are sold to serve as menial servants, with no hope of ever being freed. In developing countries greedy owners of mills and factories and large corporations employ children for a pittance to produce cheap goods to be sold for huge profits. It is not uncommon in some societies to take girls to faraway cities to sell them into prostitution. Slavery in any form, anywhere, is a sin against God.

By his preaching and writing, Paul has made us aware of where he stood on social issues. He wrote to the Ephesians and to others that in Christ there is no wall of partition. The gospel does not recognize any distinction between free and slave; all are sinners, and all are in need of a Savior. Yet Paul is also aware that as long as we live on this earth, polluted by sin, problems in human relations will exist. Differences in race, gender, nationality, economic status, and other divisive factors that draw their strength from sin will continue to plague human society. And it is Satan's studied plan to inject these differences even within the community of faith. If at all possible he would destroy the unity that ought to characterize the faith community.

Paul was fully aware of these dangers, and he writes to the Ephesians with great sensitivity. Some have misunderstood Paul's counsel to slaves and masters in Ephesians 6:5-9. They have suggested that Paul was supporting the tragedy of slavery. Nothing can be further from truth, particularly coming as it does from the apostle of universal brotherhood. What, then, is Paul saying?

Paul counsels the slaves in Ephesus to obey their masters and do their work as if they are doing it for Christ (verse 5). We must take note of Paul's mind-set at the time of this writing. The apostle is absolutely convinced that the second coming of Jesus is near, when all the consequences of sin will be eliminated and we will be citizens of the new heaven and new earth. It's only a matter of time—Christ is coming soon, and the ills of this world will be over.

With Christ's coming so near, it is essential that Christians focus on that glorious day, accepting the pain and tragedy of sin that presently govern the present life. Hence the stability of the communion of the faith—with no wall between—was the apostle's objective, not the incitement of a socioeconomic revolution. "It was not the apostle's work to overturn arbitrarily or suddenly the established order of society. To attempt this would be to prevent the success of the gospel. But he taught principles which struck at the very foundation of slavery and which, if carried into effect, would surely undermine the whole system."[6]

Further, Paul's counsel should be viewed within the context of his overall gospel scheme of social relationships, in which there is neither master nor slave. That is the ideal, and it is the apostle's hope that such an ideal would pervade every church. With that in view, Paul writes to the masters to be kind to their servants, "giving up threatening, knowing that your own Master also is in heaven, and there is no partiality with Him" (verse 9).

This itself was revolutionary counsel in Paul's time. The apostle's counsel to masters includes not only the present situation but their future destiny. Masters too are servants of the heavenly Master, and in His eyes there is no partiality. His salvation and His judgment will be meted out to this earth's masters and their slaves in the same manner. Before God there is neither master nor slave—all are sinners facing either salvation or judgment, depending on how they relate to life's great issues. Underlying the apostle's counsel to masters is a firm warning that they have a duty to relate to their slaves as Christians, not as pagans.

Paul's counsel also outlines a Christian philosophy of work. We may not all be slaves, but we are all workers in one sense or another. We work for an employer, for a wage, and whatever the conditions may be, Christians should subscribe to a high work ethic. Paul mentions several principles of this ethic. Work with sincerity, as though you work for Christ. Work "not with eyeservice, as men pleasers, but as bondservants of Christ" (verse 6). Whatever our work, we are to do it as though it is the will of God (verse 6). Work with goodwill. Work honestly, as though your reward comes from the Lord (verse 7).

No, Paul did not advocate slavery, nor did he advocate rebellion. His call was to live within the context of the cross on the one hand (in peaceful reconciliation) and of the impending Second Coming on the other (the ultimate resolution to all evils in the world). Paul knew that slaves cannot change their circumstances but that they can conquer them.

There we have a good Christian philosophy—we cannot destroy evil at the moment, but we must not let evil destroy us.

Paul's skillfully balanced Christian counsel and ministry did bear fruit, and many slave owners became ardent Christians, along with their slaves. The case of Philemon is a good example. Paul returned Onesimus, a runaway slave of Philemon's, and asked the latter to accept him "no longer as a slave but . . . as a beloved brother" (Philemon 16, RSV). From slave to a beloved brother. That, in essence, is the gospel of new relationships.

---

[1] J.R.W. Stott, *The Message of Ephesians,* p. 225.

[2] D. Martyn Lloyd-Jones, *Life in the Spirit: in Marriage, Home and Work* (Grand Rapids: Baker Books, 1973), pp. 175, 176.

[3] W. Barclay, *The Letters to the Galatians and the Ephesians,* p. 176.

[4] *The Journal of John Wesley,* quoted in John MacArthur, Jr., *The MacArthur New Testament Commentary: Ephesians,* p. 319.

[5] E. G. White, *Mind, Character, and Personality,* vol. 1, p. 156.

[6] White, *The Acts of the Apostles,* pp. 459, 460.

CHAPTER 12

The Christian Warfare

Ephesians 6:10-12

Finally, my brethren . . ."As he draws to the close of his Epistle, Paul prepares the believers for what's ahead of them. The word "finally" means "from now on." "From henceforth" is the way Paul makes the transition from what he has said thus far to what he is about to say. Thus far the apostle has sketched the moving drama of the plan of redemption and its demands on the worthy walk of the Christian. Now the apostle is ready to introduce his concluding dimension of the Christian life.

Ephesians 6:10-16 speaks about the Christian warfare with the cosmic forces that are headed by Satan. Satan's attention is focused on "the brethren"—those who have accepted the mystery of the gospel, those who have accepted the reconciliation brought by Jesus. It is to these brethren, who face the warfare "against principalities, against powers, against the rulers of the darkness of this age, against spiritual hosts of wickedness in the heavenly places" (verse 12), that the apostle provides these words of final warning and counsel.

Is this warfare real? How is it being fought on earth? Is victory assured? How are we to engage in the warfare? What is our equipment in this warfare?

The Reality of the Warfare

In one sentence the Bible underscores the reality of the warfare: "There was war in heaven" (Rev.12:7, KJV). Within the holy precincts of heaven, before the holy throne of God, in the presence of the Creator, an event occurred that is described as war in heaven. The word "war" indicates that there arose in heaven someone who was against God's will, who questioned God's role, His character, and His sovereignty. Such rebellion cannot exist in heaven, and it needed to be dealt with. Hence "there was war in heaven: Michael and his angels fought against the dragon; and the dragon fought and his angels, and prevailed not; neither was their place found any more in heaven. And the great dragon was cast out, that old serpent, called the Devil, and Satan, which deceiveth the whole world: he was cast out into the earth, and his angels were cast out with him" (verses 7-9, KJV).

This cosmic struggle between God and Satan moved from heaven to earth when Satan and his angels were cast out. Ever since, this warfare has been fought over the allegiance of the human race. On whose side shall we be—on the side of God or the on the side of the evil one? The issues behind the controversy are many and are related primarily to the character of God. Is He arbitrary or loving? Is His law beyond the ability of His creatures to obey? Can God be just and loving at the same time? How can He demand the death of the sinner and yet claim to save the sinner by His grace?

Satan challenged God's sovereignty over the universe and His right to create the worlds. He wanted to usurp God's authority (see Isa. 14:13, 14; Eze. 28:12-17; Jude 6). With selfishness turned into prideful arrogance, and with pride turned into deceitfulness, leading angels away from their loyalty to God, Satan initiated his war of disobedience and rebellion against God. It was that rebellion that led God to oust Lucifer from heaven.

Earth, the Theater of the Cosmic War

Cast out of heaven, Satan shifted his operations to earth."No longer free to stir up rebellion in heaven, Satan's enmity against God found a new field in plotting the ruin of the human race. In the happiness and peace of the holy pair in Eden he beheld a vision of the bliss that to him was forever lost. Moved by envy, he determined to incite them to disobedience, and bring upon them the guilt and penalty of sin. He would change their love to distrust and their songs of praise to reproaches against their Maker."[1]

Satan's first target was Adam and Eve. Although perfection marked the creation of Adam and Eve, God had bestowed upon them the freedom of choice. Satan took advantage of this and launched his temptation to test the loyalty of our first parents. Instead of obeying God and trusting His Word, Adam and Eve fell victims to the wiles of the devil and disobeyed God. "As by one man sin entered into the world, and death by sin; and so death passed upon all men, for that all have sinned" (Rom. 5:12, KJV).

With the fall of Adam and Eve, all humanity have become prey to Satan and participants in the great controversy between good and evil. The history of the human race has become a history of this cosmic conflict, centered on earth. Abel and Cain, the Flood, Joseph and Potiphar's wife,

Pharaoh and the children of Israel, Elijah and Jezebel, Babylon's destruction of Jerusalem, Herod's attempt to crush the infant Jesus, the temptations, Gethsemane and the Crucifixion, the persecution of the early church, the Dark Ages—these are all mileposts of the cosmic struggle, leading right up to our own time. Each of these and a thousand other stories witness to God's hand in time and history. God will not let His purposes fail or His mission collapse. But He calls upon human instruments to do His will, to stand for His service, to uphold His Word, and to resist the devil.

The closing scenes of our Lord's life are a lasting testimony to Satan's persistence and Christ's unfailing loyalty to His mission and to His Father. Gethsemane was one of the crucial battlefields of the great controversy. Satan and his entire army were arraigned against Christ, who bore the sins of the world. If only Satan could make Jesus distance Himself from the cup of atonement, the cosmic conflict would have turned into triumph for the evil one. As the fate of the universe trembled in the balance, the Son of God chose His Father's will.

Satan's defeat in Gethsemane would not lead him to concede failure. He would try again. So came the cross, and the suffering and victory of the Son there became central to God's plan for crushing the evil one. The blood of Jesus shed upon the cross was not a result of human suffering at the hands of evil men, but each drop became a fountain of divine grace for repentant sinners. There on the cross the shedding of blood completed the reconciliation of humanity with God. To everyone who accepts the power—the wonderful power—of that blood, there is reconciliation, and there is victory in the cosmic conflict.

We Are in the Warfare (Ephesians 6:10-12)

The apostle's message in Ephesians 6 is clear. "For we do not wrestle against flesh and blood, but against principalities, against powers, against the rulers of the darkness of this age, against spiritual hosts of wickedness in the heavenly places" (verse 12). Our war is real. Our war is spiritual. Our war involves not just time but eternity as well. Our objectives are well defined. Our victory is already assured if we are on the Victor's side.

Whatever the grand and cosmic issues of the great controversy, right now the unseen battle between Christ and Satan is being fought for the allegiance of the human heart and mind. Your heart and mine. "Many look on this conflict between Christ and Satan as having no special bearing on their own life; and for them it has little interest. But within the domain of every human heart this controversy is repeated. Never does one leave the ranks of evil for the service of God without encountering the assaults of Satan. The enticements which Christ resisted were those that we find it so difficult to withstand."[2]

Satan stands ever ready to deceive us and draw us away from the love and power of God. He fights for the mind of each person on earth with his masterful, deceptive skills. Therefore, the apostle gives us a stirring call: "Put on the whole armor of God that you may be able to stand against the wiles of the devil. Put on the whole armor of God that you may be able to stand against the wiles of the devil" (verse 11).

"Be strong in the Lord and in the power of His might" (verse 10). Before mentioning the Christian armor with which we are to engage in the warfare against evil, Paul wants us to make sure on whose side our spiritual allegiance is. "Be strong in the Lord" is his opening salvo. Unless we make sure where we stand and from whom our strength comes, we do not even have a starting point in the spiritual warfare. Our strength comes from the Lord. Not from ourselves, not from anything we have achieved, not in our intellectual strength, not even in our understanding of the doctrine of Christian life and duty. All these are important, but first and foremost we must know our Lord personally, intimately, continually.

At the beginning of his letter Paul prayed that the believers should be aware of "the exceeding greatness of His power toward us who believe, according to the working of His mighty power which He worked in Christ when He raised Him from the dead and seated Him at His right hand in the heavenly places, far above all principality and power and might and dominion" (Eph. 1:19-21).

Note the mighty strength that flows from God. It is God's power that worked in Christ and raised Him from the dead. It is God's power that caused Him to ascend to the heavens victorious over sin and Satan. It is God's power that put Jesus on the right hand of the Father's throne. If we have this power as the source of our strength, no evil force can have a hold on us in our spiritual battle. The empowering of Jesus is so complete that those who trust in Him need not be afraid of all the craftiness of Satan.

Satan may tempt, but his temptations have no power over the one who abides in the strength of God. Consider Joseph. His honesty, intellectual strength, discernment of issues, and moral uprightness elevated him to be in charge of Potiphar's household. For a slave to reach such a high and noble place was a great achievement indeed. But not for a moment did Joseph think that all his achievements were because of his power and strength. He was always conscious that what and who he was came from God, in whom he chose to abide.

But Satan was waiting, ready to trap Joseph. The trap came in the form of a beautiful and willing woman who "day by day" enticed him to cross the forbidden frontier. The beauty of a willing partner, the safety of a secretive bed, and the whisper of the great tempter were all directed at Joseph. But nothing could break his will or tempt him into yielding to Egypt's beauty. His strength was in God: "How then can I do this great wickedness, and sin against God?" (Gen. 39:9).

To Joseph, the issue was not just illicit sex; the issue was the choice between God and Satan. It was a costly choice, for it landed him in jail. True discipleship is always costly, but in the strength of the Lord the disciple comes out victorious. Joseph was a good man, but before he was good he was a godly man. In the Lord—always and continuously—you can resist evil and engage Satan victoriously. Hence the apostle's counsel: "Be strong in the Lord and in the power of His might."Against a believer who is clothed with that strength and that power there can stand no foe.

Paul continues: "Put on the whole armor of God, that you may be able to stand against the wiles of the devil" (verse 11). For a moment follow Paul's logic and spiritual burden. Our warfare is not against flesh and blood. We are not to involve ourselves in any struggle against human beings, including unbelievers. Indeed, we are called to "live peaceably with all men" (Rom. 12:18). Our warfare is against spiritual forces of darkness.

Paul uses the word "wrestle," as if to emphasize that we are involved in hand-to-hand combat with the devil and his cohorts. Satan may not attack us openly, though that possibility must not be discounted. He is more sophisticated; he may even appear as an "angel of light" (2 Cor. 11:14). He is a dangerous wolf who disguises himself as a sheep to attack the fold of the Good Shepherd (John 10:12).

Satan's tactics are called the "wiles of the devil." Wile indicates cunningness. Satan presents darkness as light, mixes error with truth, causes indifference to truth as a matter of no consequence, leads us to neglect the study of God's Word and prayer. He represents the role of grace as freedom to do anything, and even describes God's law as irrelevant. We see these wiles in action all around us, both within and outside the church. No Christian is safe from these deceptions until he or she is strongly and firmly rooted in God's Word and claims the strength of God's Spirit.

Hence Paul counsels the believers to action as they face their spiritual warfare: Stand! Take up arms! Put on armor! Be strong! This is no time for vacillation. This is the time to be strong in the Lord, to be empowered by His Word. "Wherever we are, whatever our circumstances, whatever we have done, whatever we have to do, there is never a holiday in the spiritual realm."[3]

The apostle James's counsel is timely: "Therefore submit to God. Resist the devil and he will flee from you. Draw near to God and He will draw near to you. Cleanse your hands, you sinners; and purify your hearts, you double-minded. Lament and mourn and weep! Let your laughter be turned to mourning and your joy to gloom. Humble yourselves in the sight of the Lord, and He will lift you up" (James 4:7-10).

The spiritual conditions that we face are serious. We cannot take things lightly. Therefore, the apostle warns us to "put on the whole armor of God." The emphasis on "whole" should not be missed. The battle is all-encompassing, aimed at our body, mind, spirit, and soul, our relationship and fellowship, our present and future. Therefore, our preparedness and our armor must be complete.

Paul mentions at least six weapons that make up the armor, and not one can be neglected. All are forged and furnished by God as one unit; and we cannot afford to neglect one without weakening the whole. "The Christian is vulnerable at many spots, and often that characteristic he thinks is his strongest turns out, under temptation, to be his weakest. As a chain is no stronger than its weakest link, so the Christian is no stronger than his weakest element of character. In view of the variety of foes that must be met and the various weaknesses of the flesh, nothing less than the entire armor will suffice."[4]

---

[1] Ellen G. White, *Patriarchs and Prophets* (Mountain View, Calif.: Pacific Press Pub. Assn., 1890), p. 52.

[2] White, *The Desire of Ages,* p. 116.

[3] D. Martyn Lloyd-Jones, *The Christian Soldier* (Grand Rapids: Baker Books, 1977), p. 175.

[4] *The Seventh-day Adventist Bible Commentary,* vol. 6, p. 1044.

CHAPTER 13

The Christian Armor

Ephesians 6:13-18

In the Christian life the call to arms is as real as the call to peace. While Christ calls the tired and heavy-laden, the sick and sin-burdened, to receive from Him respite and rest (Matt. 11:28), He also warns them that Christian discipleship is not a journey of ease. It is a battle and a march. Nowhere is this described as clearly as in Ephesians 6:12, 13.

Our part in this spiritual warfare is not to be colored by fear or pessimism. We are to be strong in the Lord and to claim the victory Christ has already won (Eph. 1:19, 20). But if we already have a part in that victory, what is the necessity for the battle? The answer is found in the nature of the Christian faith and the deceitfulness of the devil.

The moment we accept Jesus, that very moment we are forgiven our sins; we are justified—that is, we stand before God as though we had never sinned. That is because of what Christ has done on our behalf. But justification is only the first step. It must be followed by sanctification—the process of being made holy, more and more like our Savior. Sanctification is a lifelong process. As we pursue that process in faith, God is on our side. His power is with us. We are not alone.

But at the same time "your adversary the devil walks about like a roaring lion, seeking whom he may devour" (1 Peter 5:8). The path to sanctification is filled with the devil's traps, and it is here that our spiritual warfare takes on its ferocity. Martyn Lloyd-Jones has some comforting words for the saints who are engaged in this spiritual warfare: "We have got to realize, as we fight this fight of faith and wrestle with these principalities and powers and face the assaults of the world and the flesh and the devil, that God is involved in it with us. We would never have been in it but for that. The ultimate battle is the battle between God and the devil, between heaven and hell, between light and darkness. . . . This campaign cannot fail, because God's honour is involved in it."[1]

The battle is the Lord's. The victory is His. We are His soldiers, called upon to be strong, to stand, and to put on the entire armor of God. Just because Christ has won the victory and offers it to us does not mean that we are freed from fighting the devil. We are called upon to "stand against the wiles of the devil" (Eph. 6:11), and "take up the whole armor of God . . . and having done all, to stand" (verse 13).

In these words of great significance, can you hear the bugle call? Can you hear the trumpets sound? Can you hear the great Commander's charge? On to the battle! Never look back! Fight with all your might, for your might is the strength of the Lord! Victory is yours.

The apostle wants us to make sure that we are clothed fully "with the whole armor of God." He mentions six components of the armor. Not one is to be neglected. Together they comprise God's armor, not ours. In the strength of that armor we are to go to the battle. "It is God alone who knows your enemy, and He knows exactly the provision that is essential to you if you are to continue standing. Every single part and portion of this armor is absolutely essential; and the first thing you have to learn is that you are not in a position to pick and choose."[2]

Now we are ready to examine the parts of this armor.

The Girdle of Truth (Ephesians 6:13, 14)

Paul is writing this Epistle from a Roman jail, ever under the watchful eye of a Roman soldier. Day in and day out the apostle is conscious of the soldier. Soldiers came and left in shifts, but there was one thing common to them—their armor. The armor was a symbol of loyalty to the emperor; it represented the soldier's readiness to do the emperor's bidding.

The apostle could not miss the obvious lessons, and envisions every Christian to be a soldier—fully clothed with the armor of God, loyal to His calling, ready to do His service. From this daily encounter with the Roman guards in their full armor Paul draws the analogy and applies it to the greater warfare, to a more supreme Leader.

The apostle first notes the girdle for the waist—truth. The Roman soldier wore an outer tunic that served as his primary clothing. It covered the body loosely. Loose clothing can be an impediment in battle, so it was held close to the body by a belt. The belt also provided a support to hold his sword.

Peter also used the analogy: "Therefore gird up the loins of your mind, be sober, and rest your hope fully upon the grace that is to be brought to you at the revelation of Jesus Christ" (1 Peter 1:13). Paul equates this "girding up the loins" with wearing the belt of truth in preparation for the spiritual warfare.

What is this truth that guards us against all evil? First and foremost, the truth is our Lord Himself (John 14:6). Being girded with truth means being totally committed to Jesus. What He says we obey. Where He commands we go. What He does, we do. Anything contrary to His will we reject. With such unconditional, uncompromising commitment to Jesus preparing us to face the devil we too can say as He did, "The prince of this world cometh, and hath nothing in me" (verse 30, KJV).

Many people, including Christians, have wrong ideas of truth. Some say truth is a logical proposition. If a = b and b = c, then a = c. That is true in mathematics and logic, but it is not the kind of truth that can keep the devil away.

Others would say that truth is whatever works. I have a Toyota Corolla. It works. It takes me from place A to place B, and as far as my transportation needs are concerned, it is a great vehicle. If that is truth, Satan has no argument with it at all. Still others would say truth is relative—it all depends. What appears as good for the upbringing of my child is not necessarily appropriate for my neighbor's child. It all depends on circumstances, emotions, and relationships. That may be an observable fact, but such facts do not collectively or singly make truth.

Scientists would say that what is testable and repeatable is truth. Two parts of hydrogen and one part of oxygen when mixed together produce water. That was the case yesterday and today, and will be tomorrow. But it is not the same as saying that Jesus is truth yesterday, today, and forever. Truth is not even a religious proposition. When I say that I believe in God, it is not necessarily truth. The question is What kind of God? The answers are many and variable, and all cannot be truth.

Truth is revelation—God's revelation. To a Christian who wants to be victorious in life's spiritual battles, the ultimate truth is in the person of Jesus. It is in Him that the fullness of God and His truth are revealed. The truth that is Jesus is a saving, redeeming truth. It calls for death to sin (Rom. 6:1-4) and for a life of righteousness, moral integrity, spiritual coherence, and a faithfulness to God's expectations in all relationships.

Only unreserved commitment to Christ can arm a person to truth-seeking and truth-telling, and truth-living in a world of sin. Hence Paul's admonition: "Put on the Lord Jesus Christ, and make no provision for the flesh, to fulfill its lusts" (Rom. 13:14).

As noted earlier, a Roman soldier used a belt to hold up his outer clothing, reducing impediment to his warfare; similarly, Christ helps secure us for battle. Jesus the truth must cover our entire being so that our humanness does not hinder our spiritual warfare. Our talk and our walk, our worship and our work, our emotions and our intellect, our relationships and pursuits—all must be held firm by the truth that is Jesus.

There is another aspect to truth that should not be neglected. Truth as it is in Jesus is revealed through the Scriptures. Jesus is the incarnate Word. Scriptures are the inspired word. Both are essential for us to understand and be equipped in the path we should trod. "All Scripture is given by inspiration of God, and is profitable for doctrine, for reproof, for correction, for instruction in righteousness, that the man of God may be complete, thoroughly equipped for every good work" (2 Tim. 3:16, 17).

Without a full knowledge and practice of biblical doctrine and teaching, the apostle warns, we will be "tossed to and fro and carried about with every wind of doctrine, by the trickery of men, in the cunning craftiness of deceitful plotting" (Eph. 4:14). "If the truth of God be not deep rooted in the heart, you cannot stand the test of temptation. There is only one power that can keep us steadfast under the most trying circumstances—the grace of God in truth."[3]

Having Jesus and following the Scriptures will lead the Christian into another important aspect of truth as part of the armor. That is, a life of truthfulness. If we walk according to what Jesus commanded us and what the Bible demands of us, we will be honest and truthful in all that we do—in what we speak, what we listen to, and how we relate in our work and in our relationships. No lie will come out of a Christian's lips. No deceit will dwell in his or her heart.

"God requires 'truth in the inward being,' and the Christian must at all costs be honest and truthful [Ps. 51:6; Eph. 4:15, 25]. To be deceitful, to lapse into hypocrisy, to resort to intrigue and scheming, this is to play the devil's game, and we shall not be able to beat him at his own game. What he abominates is transparent truth. He loves darkness; light causes him to flee. For spiritual as for mental health honesty about oneself is indispensable."[4]

One final point on wearing the belt of truth. A Roman soldier not wearing a belt was considered off-duty. Is there a time in the Christian life when we can consider ourselves off-duty? Is there a time when the truth of "putting on Jesus" and living a life of moral and spiritual integrity becomes optional?

The Breastplate of Righteousness (Ephesians 6:14)

Made of heavy metal, the breastplate covered the torso from neck to hip, protecting vital organs of the body. In ancient times Jews often equated the heart as the seat of human thought and emotions. Satan's attack is particularly aimed to distort our mind and pollute our emotions. A mind disobedient to God is easily attracted to an evil lifestyle.

Evil lifestyle does not necessarily mean degradation at its worst or immorality in the worst imaginable way. Satan is satisfied if he can just divert the mind from surrender to indifference, from ways of righteousness to neglect of truth. He does not necessarily want our emotions to dwell on altars of evil, such as pornography; he is satisfied if we can only exchange love for lust, care for abuse, spiritual uprightness for mere good deeds. Hence it is important to protect our mind and emotions and every vital organ of spiritual life with the breastplate of righteousness.

Righteousness, of course, does not mean self-righteousness, for that is the worst kind of sin. Satan would love for us to engage in it, and pretend it is our weapon of defense. In the eyes of God "we are all like an unclean thing, and all our righteousnesses are like filthy rags" (Isa. 64:6). Nor is righteousness rightdoing, although a person with the breastplate of righteousness will do that which is right.

What Paul means by righteousness is the putting aside of our self-centered, self-righteous, and sinful ways and the putting on of the righteousness that comes from Christ. In Romans 3:21-26 we find a definition of the righteousness that comes from God: 1. The righteousness of God is revealed apart from the law. It does not come from our good works. 2. It was witnessed to by the Old Testament. 3. It is given to all who believe in Jesus Christ. 4. It leads to our being justified freely through God's grace in Jesus Christ. 5. It is demonstrated through the blood of Jesus.

That is the Pauline definition of the righteousness that serves as our breastplate of protection against the wily attacks of Satan. In telling us to put on this breastplate the apostle is exhorting us to put on Christ and His righteousness. Christ our righteousness—the pledge of the new covenant—becomes our eternal protection. When Christ dwells in us, Satan finds no room in our lives.

"All who have put on the robe of Christ's righteousness will stand before Him as chosen and faithful and true. Satan has no power to pluck them out of the hand of the Savior. Not one soul who in penitence and faith has claimed His protection will Christ permit to pass under the enemy's power."[5]

The Shoes of the Gospel of Peace (Ephesians 6:15)

Shoes may seem a humble part of one's attire, but they are important. As a 10-year-old I lived in a crowded neighborhood in a small town. Very few people had shoes, and those who did saved them for special occasions such as a church service or a wedding. Some wore rubber slippers that were uncomfortable in the hot and humid weather. But the majority walked barefoot. One of these was my friend's father. Each night he walked barefoot to work in a factory three miles from home. One morning I noticed him limping. My friend and I asked him what had happened. "Oh, nothing much," he answered. "I must have stepped on a thorn or a nail or something sharp. It should be OK."

But it was not OK. The poor man could not afford to see a doctor. Days passed, and the wound did not heal. Within weeks he died. My friend lost his father, and neither of us could understand how such deadly danger could have lurked in a nail or a thorn. During the funeral service we heard such words as "rusted nail," "gangrene," and "no immediate treatment" whispered. A pair of footwear could have prevented a needless tragedy. Shoes for the feet are important.

Roman soldiers wore boots with studded nails on the soles to ensure good traction during battle. A soldier cannot afford to slide or fall when locked in deadly combat. Likewise, Christians need to stand firm and unshakable in the gospel truth in order to ensure victory.

Why is the gospel of peace likened to shoes? Two meanings are possible. First, the gospel has brought peace to the Christian: "Therefore, having been justified by faith, we have peace with God through our Lord Jesus Christ" (Rom. 5:1). The peace we experience through Jesus is peace with God and with our fellow beings. With that peace we stand free from guilt; we stand in the confidence that God will fight with us in our battles. "If God is for us, who can be against us?" (Rom. 8:31).

The gospel of peace, in addition to bringing about a reconciled relationship, calls us to be bearers of the good news. Perhaps the apostle had the beautiful passage of Isaiah 52:7 in mind: "How beautiful upon the mountains are the feet of him who brings good news, who proclaims peace, who brings glad tidings of good things, who proclaims salvation, who says to Zion, 'Your God reigns!' " In what better way can a Christian soldier carry on his or her battle for the Lord than by proclaiming to those who have not heard the good news of the gospel: "Your God reigns!" This is a message that the devil trembles to hear.

An inactive Christian cannot be a victor in spiritual warfare. The

Samaritan woman found peace and at once rushed to share it with her villagers (John 4:28, 29). The invalid at the Pool of Bethesda found peace and healing in Jesus and did not hesitate to bear witness (John 5:11-14). Johannes Blauw describes it well: "Missionary work is like a pair of sandals that have been given to the church in order that it shall set out on the road and keep on going to make known the mystery of the gospel."[6]

The Shield of Faith (Ephesians 6:16)

Paul introduces the shield with the phrase "above all." It does not mean "most important of all the weapons," but rather "besides these" or "in addition to." The apostle has no favorite piece of Christian armory. All are important; none may be neglected or set aside.

The Roman shield was of two kinds. One was small, perhaps two feet in diameter. This was tied to the arm by two leather straps; the soldier moved it back and forth to ward off oncoming missiles. The second was larger, about two and a half feet wide and four and a half feet high. Designed to protect the entire body, it was made of solid wood and covered with a sheet of metal or heavy leather. Soldiers crouched behind these shields during battle, to guard against the enemy's arrows and spears. Quite a protective weapon.

What is this faith that acts as our shield? Is it a belief in (as in a person) or belief about (as in a logical proposition or fact)? Is it an act of reason or an act of will? Is it a mental assent or a basic trust? Many such questions confront us when we consider what faith is about. But one thing we can be sure of: "Without faith it is impossible to please Him, for he who comes to God must believe that He is, and that He is a rewarder of those who diligently seek Him" (Heb. 11:6).

Out of this simple passage emerge several fundamental truths of what faith is all about. 1. Faith involves an a priori—that God exists. The existence of God is not open for debate, dialogue, or experimentation. God is faith's first axiom. 2. Faith involves a personal trust in God. 3. Faith is the instrument through which we can draw near to God—not through our works, not through our skills, but through simple faith that God is. 4. Faith is essential to know and to please God. We do not choose the way to please Him; we are simply to follow the ways He has suggested that would please Him. 5. The reward of faith is in the object of faith itself. That is, God is the rewarder of faith.

"Faith is trusting God—believing that He loves us and knows best what is for our good. Thus, instead of our own, it leads us to choose His way. In place of our ignorance, it accepts His wisdom; in place of our weakness, His strength; in place of our sinfulness, His righteousness. Our lives, ourselves, are already His; faith acknowledges His ownership and accepts its blessing. Truth, uprightness, purity, have been pointed out as secrets of life's success. It is faith that puts us in possession of these principles."[7]

The story is told of a missionary who was translating the Bible into one of the dialects of the South Sea islands. He came to the word "faith," and was frustrated that no one in the tribe could come up with a word to define it. He spent several days talking to many people, but didn't find the right word. One day a native of the island came into the missionary's house after a hard day's work and after walking a long distance. He literally threw himself onto a large sofa, saying, "It feels good to rest my whole weight on the sofa." The missionary caught that phrase and used it to translate faith as "placing one's whole weight on God."

God is able to bear all your weight and give you rest. That's really the end result of trusting in Him. When faith as a basic, implicit, unwavering trust in God controls our lives, it empowers us "to quench all fiery darts of the evil one" (Eph. 6:16).

Those flaming darts come in different forms—temptation, doubt, lust, despair, trials, rebellion, guilt, etc. Whatever the dart, the shield of faith is strong enough to repel it. Faith in an unfailing God provides us with absolute confidence to withstand Satan. God Himself "is a shield to those who put their trust in Him" (Prov. 30:5).

The Helmet of Salvation (Ephesians 6:17)

The helmet is a life-protecting device. It is designed to safeguard the head from danger. I think of Albert. He was young, handsome, intelligent, and very promising. He was the delight of his parents, and a blessing to the small church community with whom he shared his love of music, his computer skills, and his knowledge of the Bible. Children sought after him. Adults knew that he would grow to be someone they would be proud of. But on the day he turned 18 disaster struck Albert, plunging his parents into grief and the little Adventist community into unbearable sorrow. Within minutes after leaving home to run an errand, a speeding truck hit Albert's motorcycle from behind, and he landed on his head."Severe head wounds," the autopsy surgeon said. "If only he had been wearing a helmet."

A helmet safeguards the head. In many parts of the world the law requires the wearing of a helmet as a protection against various hazards. In

Paul's time a helmet, made of tough metal such as bronze or iron, was standard gear for soldiers. No sword could cut through it.

So it is in Christian warfare. Believers must put on their helmet to protect the seat of their will, where momentous decisions are made. Paul identifies that helmet as salvation from sin. In 1 Thessalonians 5:8 Paul adds that our helmet is "the hope of salvation."

But the question that often troubles the Christian is How can I have the assurance of salvation? The answer is not in us but in God. The emphasis on God's work in the life of a Christian (1 Cor. 12:6, 11; Gal. 2:8; Eph. 1:11, 20) gives us the assurance that the contours of salvation—the beginning, the continuation, and the culmination—are guaranteed by God's grace to everyone who believes in Him and walks with Him.

Karl Barth once noted: "It is God who gives each one whatever he accomplishes in 'working out his salvation.'. . . As such we put ourselves entirely into the power of God, that as such we recognize that all grace, that everything—the willing and the accomplishing, the beginning and the end, the faith and the revelation, the questions and the answers, the seeking and the finding—comes from God and is reality only in God. . . . Man cannot put his salvation into practice except as he recognizes: it is *God!*"[8]

That is the beauty of the gospel. God is paramount in salvation. His grace initiates and completes the redemptive process. "Whatever is to be done at His command may be accomplished in His strength. All His biddings are enablings."[9] God is at work in us.

God's grace is His activity to reconcile us to Himself, to make us a part of the family of God. Having come into the family, we live in the family, bearing fruits of God's love through the power of His amazing grace. Staying in God's family is the basis of our assurance. Hence, put on the helmet of salvation—the experience of salvation now and the hope of final redemption when Christ returns the second time.

Satan shall not shake the assurance that we have in Christ, for He is our assurance (1 Peter 1:3-10; Rom. 8:31-39; John 6:37-39). Doubt and discouragement will not sway our experience. Instead, joy and fellowship with the Spirit guarantee our assurance here and our inheritance in the home to come (Eph. 1:14). "God's saving power is our only defense against the enemy of our souls."[10]

The Sword of the Spirit (Ephesians 6:17)

The first five weapons of God's armor—girdle of truth, breastplate of righteousness, shoes of the gospel, shield of faith, and the helmet of salvation—are defensive in nature. They are weapons of protection against Satan's onslaughts. Now the apostle comes to the final weapon, an offensive one: "the sword of the Spirit, which is the word of God" (Eph. 6:17).

By relating the Word of God to the Spirit the apostle identifies the origin of the Word. The Bible is not a human document. Its origin is to be located in the mind of God. The apostle makes this clear elsewhere: "All Scripture is given by inspiration of God, and is profitable for doctrine, for reproof, for correction, for instruction in righteousness, that the man of God may be complete, thoroughly equipped for every good work" (2 Tim. 3:16, 17).

What does "inspiration" mean? The secularist would call the Bible inspired in the sense that Shakespeare's plays or Milton's poems may be inspired. That is, they move, excite, elevate, console. But that's not what the Bible means by "inspiration." The Greek word *theopneustos* actually means "breathed out by God"—not so much in-spired as ex-pired. Thus the text explicitly teaches the divine origin of the Scriptures. God breathed out the Scriptures, and metaphorically, we might say the Scriptures are God's breath.

This thought is extended and enforced by a striking argument in 2 Peter 1:19-21. There the Scriptures are presented as more sure than the eyewitness account of the apostle. Peter was convinced that they are not a result of any "private interpretation" or of any human endeavor but a result of God's revelatory initiative. Ellen White said, "The creative energy that called the worlds into existence is in the word of God. This word imparts power; it begets life."[11]

Thus the Bible is not only God's self-disclosure but also God's instrument to enrich, guide, and govern us in our pursuit of the Christian life and its warfare. Accepting God's Word as the power of the Spirit enables us with answers to life's crucial issues—Who am I? Where did I come from? Where am I going? What is the meaning of history? What happens at death? How does God relate to me? How am I to relate to others, to the world at large? The Bible has something to say on these questions; as Christians we need the right answers to face the devil when he confronts us with doubts and contradictions on such major issues.

Thomas Guthrie, a Scottish pastor, has powerfully stated what the Bible ought to mean to the Christian: "The Bible is an armory of heavenly weapons, a laboratory of infallible medicines, a mine of exhaustless wealth. It is a guidebook for every road, a chart for every sea, a medicine for every malady, and a balm for every wound. Rob us of our Bible, and our sky has lost its sun."[12]

Jesus provides a perfect example of how to use the Word in our warfare against Satan. Each temptation in the wilderness aimed at leading Jesus either to doubt or to test the promises of God's Word. The temptations were strong and fierce. But Jesus' defense was stronger than Satan's attack. His defense lay in an abiding trust in God's Word.

But to know the Word is not enough. Satan too knows the Scripture—to cheat and defraud. The power of God is available only when the soul surrenders unconditionally to the demands of that Word. Doubt about God's Word is a sharp weapon in Satan's arsenal. He tried it successfully with Adam and Eve, and he tried it again with the Second Adam, Jesus. But Jesus overcame each of the devil's temptations by using God's Word.

"Jesus met Satan with the words of Scripture. 'It is written,' He said. In every temptation the weapon of His warfare was the word of God. Satan demanded of Christ a miracle as a sign of His divinity. But that which is greater than all miracles, a firm reliance upon a 'Thus saith the Lord,' was a sign that could not be controverted. So long as Christ held to this position, the tempter could gain no advantage."[13]

So it may be with us. Says the psalmist, "Your word I have hidden in my heart, that I might not sin against You!" (Ps. 119:11). To this add the promise provided by the author of Hebrews: "For the word of God is living and powerful, and sharper than any two-edged sword, piercing even to the division of soul and spirit, and of joints and marrow, and is a discerner of the thoughts and intents of the heart" (Heb. 4:12). When Christian soldiers use this sharp two-edged sword of the Spirit to fend off Satan's attacks, they will win the battle.

Pray Always (Ephesians 6:18)

Prayer is universal to all religions, but there is a difference between biblical prayer and other forms of prayer. The former is a response to a promise of a personal God; the latter are petitions to an impersonal, speculative force or ideology. The former is a dialogue, the latter a monologue. Prayer is speaking with God, listening to His voice, kneeling in surrender, rising up in full empowerment in God's strength. It demands nothing of ourselves—except to deny self, lean on His strength, and await upon Him. Out of that waiting flows the power with which we can walk the Christian journey and fight the spiritual warfare.

Although Paul does not list prayer as part of the armor, he does point out that none of the six parts of the armor can become our defense without prayer. Prayer precedes putting on the armor, it holds the armor in place, and it enables the armor to crush the enemy.

Paul considers prayer so important in the Christian life and warfare that he lists six great principles: "pray always"; "pray with supplication in the Spirit"; "pray in the Spirit"; "pray watchfully"; "pray with perseverance"; "pray for all the saints" (see Eph. 6:18). Effective prayer is self-denying, Spirit-filled. Paul adds that our prayers should be intercessory, pleading for the needs of others. He concludes this thought with the request for prayer for himself, an "ambassador" for the gospel (verse 20).

The importance of prayer in spiritual life cannot be overemphasized. Moses spent 40 days on Mount Sinai, praying for God's guidance in leading Israel to the Promised Land (Ex. 24:18; 34:28). Elijah prayed on Mount Carmel that fire would descend from heaven and burn up his sacrifice, publicly confirming that the God of Israel is the true God (1 Kings 18). Daniel prayed for angels to protect him from the lions' den as a testimony of the power and the saving assurance of his God (Dan. 6:20-24). David said, "Evening and morning and at noon I will pray, and cry aloud, and He shall hear my voice" (Ps. 55:17).

Jesus taught us the model prayer (Matt. 6:9-13). He prayed in Gethsemane, sweating drops of blood, in preparation for the final warfare on the cross (Matt. 26:36; Mark 14:32). The early believers prayed continually (Acts 10:2). Paul often urged the believers to pray ceaselessly (Rom. 12:12; Phil. 4:6; Col. 4:2). "Prayer," says Ellen White, "is one of the most essential duties. Without it you cannot maintain a Christian walk. It elevates, strengthens, and ennobles; it is the soul talking with God."[14]

In *Pilgrim's Progress* John Bunyan describes a moving scene in which the pilgrim Christian encounters Apollyon in the great Valley of Humiliation. Apollyon, symbolic of demonic forces that are out to crush the saints on their way to God's kingdom, attacks Christian with every weapon at his command. Armed with the sword of the Spirit, Christian puts up a valiant fight. In the midst of the deadly combat Christian loses his sword. Just as Apollyon rejoices that Christian's doom is sealed, Christian turns to another tested weapon called All-prayer, and the battle is joined again.

The persistent pilgrim uses this weapon skillfully. Suddenly his hand lights on the hilt of the sword. Wielding the sword of the Spirit with great vigor supplied by All-prayer, Christian defeats Apollyon and raises a powerful shout of victory!

Prayer is not only a fundamental essential to Christian daily living; it also carries an eschatological dimension. That is to say, prayer supplies not only strength for today but also hope for the coming end-time trials. A life girded with the armor of God—truth, righteousness, peace, faith, salvation, and the Word—and linked with Him in prayer will be victorious over the evil one.

---

[1] D. M. Lloyd-Jones, *The Christian Soldier*, p. 28.

[2] *Ibid.*, p. 179.

[3] Ellen G. White, *My Life Today* (Washington, D.C.: Review and Herald Pub. Assn., 1952), p. 310.

[4] J.R.W. Stott, *The Message of Ephesians*, pp. 277, 278.

[5] Ellen G. White, *God's Amazing Grace* (Washington, D.C.: Review and Herald Pub. Assn., 1973), p. 31.

[6] Stott, p. 280.

[7] White, *Education*, p. 253.

[8] Karl Barth, *The Epistle to the Philippians*, trans. James W. Latch (Richmond: John Knox Press, 1962), pp. 73, 74.

[9] White, *Christ's Object Lessons*, p. 333.

[10] Stott, p. 282.

[11] White, *Education*, p. 126.

[12] Thomas Guthrie, in John MacArthur, Jr., *The MacArthur New Testament Commentary: Ephesians*, p. 368.

[13] White, *The Desire of Ages*, p. 120.

[14] White, *Testimonies for the Church*, vol. 2, p. 313.

Conclusion

Ephesians 6:19-24

Paul draws his Epistle to the church in Ephesus to a close with a note of confidence, community, and charity. Not once does the Epistle reflect any bitterness over Paul's imprisonment in the Roman prison. Nor is there any animosity for the Jewish leaders who were responsible for his wrongful arrest in Jerusalem. Personal things counted very little for the apostle. He was a person of great and noble stature. He had a character dipped in pure gold, polished always by heavenly graces. If ever there was any burden on his heart, it was always the gospel of Jesus Christ, his calling to be an apostle to the Gentiles, and his concern for his fellow believers. All three blended well in this Epistle.

Confidence (Ephesians 6:19, 20)

At the end of his discussion of the Christian armor (Eph. 6:11-18) the apostle pleads with the believers to be prayer-minded at all times. Prayer for one's self, for one another, for the expanding work of the gospel, and for preparation for the final end must occupy both the individual Christian and the community of faith.

Along with this plea the apostle adds a personal note. He could have asked for numerous items to lighten his imprisonment or make his stay there a little more comfortable. Instead, he asks the Ephesians to pray for this "ambassador in chains" (verse 20). There's something extraordinary about this. A person who has experienced a true, genuine, personal call from the Lord can never forget it. With Paul, the Damascus experience ever bonded him to the One who called him. The apostle does not ask prayers for himself as a prisoner but as an ambassador of the King of kings.

Never mind the chains. His tongue is free. His mind is fresh. His heart is bubbling with joy. His discovery of the gospel is as fresh as though it happened yesterday. So the apostle looks for the day when the freedom to preach may once again be his, that he "may speak boldly" as he "ought to speak" (verse 20). An ambassador has a message to deliver. To be silent when he ought to be speaking is not an option.

What's more, he is an ambassador of the greatest thing that has happened in human history—the revelation of the "mystery of the gospel" (verse 19), the creation of one people out of many shattered pieces of humanity. It is this proclamation that there was neither Jew nor Gentile that led to Paul's arrest in Jerusalem, and it must be with that proclamation he must die. What better privilege can a Christian ask for than to face the end of life with the name of Jesus on one's lips and with the confidence of an ultimate new and united creation in one's heart? So the apostle pleads with the Ephesians: "Pray for me."

Community (Ephesians 6:21, 22)

Paul also includes in his conclusion the idea of a new community that the cross of Christ has achieved. That has been the burden of the Epistle—Paul's gospel of new relationships. Throughout the book he has spoken about the theology of this gospel and its practical implications. Now, as if to physically embrace and publicly pronounce his commitment to this idea of new community, Paul sends the letter by the hands of a man called Tychicus.

The apostle introduces his emissary as "a beloved brother, and faithful minister in the Lord" (Eph. 6:21). Tychicus is a personal confidant who will tell the Ephesians all the news about the apostle. He is a person whom Paul trusts. Before the Damascus experience the apostle would not have said any such thing about Tychicus, for Tychicus was a Gentile. But in Christ crucified Paul saw all the walls between Jews and Gentiles collapse (Eph. 2:14-18), a mystery to which the apostle became the primary steward. That made all the difference. The labels of both Jew and Gentile have given way to the only label that counts: a new creation in Christ Jesus. Such inclusiveness testifies to the power and the glory of the gospel of reconciliation.

Charity (Ephesians 6:23, 24)

The apostle began the Epistle with the words "grace," "love," and "peace" (Eph. 1:1-4). He closes the Epistle with the same words (Eph. 6:23, 24). Of the three, love expresses most poignantly, and indeed summarizes, the theme of the Epistle that all believers are one in Christ and must live in love. That's what Christian charity means. Those who live out that charity are the ones who practice the gospel of new relationships that God in Jesus Christ has inaugurated. They are chosen in Him. Therefore "grace be with all those who love our Lord Jesus Christ in sincerity. Amen" (verse 24).